PART-TIME FACULTY PERSONNEL MANAGEMENT POLICIES

PART-TIME FACULTY PERSONNEL MANAGEMENT POLICIES

George E. Biles, Ph.D., APD, CCP
Professor of Management
The American University

Howard P. Tuckman, Ph.D.
Distinguished Professor of Economics
Memphis State University

American Council on Education • Macmillan Publishing Company
NEW YORK

Collier Macmillan Publishers
LONDON

Macmillan Publishing Company
A Division of Macmillan, Inc.
866 Third Avenue, New York, N. Y. 10022

Collier Macmillan Canada, Inc.

Library of Congress Catalog Card Number: 85-31844

Printed in the United States of America

printing number
1   2   3   4   5   6   7   8   9   10

Library of Congress Cataloging in Publication Data

Biles, George E.
    Part-time faculty personnel management policies.

    (The American Council on Education/Macmillan series in higher education)
    Bibliography: p.
    Includes index
    1. College teachers, Part-time—United States.
2. Universities and colleges—United States-Administration.   I. Tuckman, Howard P.   II. Title.   III. Series.
LB2331.72.B54   1986   378'.12'0973   85-31844
ISBN 0-02-903500-7 (Macmillan)

Contents

Preface

The authors wish to thank a number of persons and institutions for giving them the opportunity to complete their work and for contributing to the quality of this book. Dr. Biles thanks the American University's Kogod College of Business Administration for granting him a one-semester sabbatical to work on this project and the American Council on Education (ACE), particularly Dr. Jerry Miller, for providing him with an office and support services. He also acknowledges the help of Dr. Tom Emmet of ACE and Regis College who acted as editor for two drafts of the manuscript. Dr. Tuckman thanks the Fogelman College of Business and Economics at Memphis State University for making the time available for him to work on this book. He would also like to thank the Ford Foundation for the initial funding that made his work on part-timers possible and both the American Association of University Professors (AAUP) and ACE staff for their many helpful discussions of the issues. He is indebted to the many administrators, faculty, and other staff who attended the joint AAUP–ACE workshops on part-timers and who made valuable observations on the academic environment and the ways in which part-timers ought to be treated. Finally, he thanks Helen Dismukes for typing the manuscript.

A host of other educational institutions with familiar acronyms—CUPA, AAJCC, AAHE, ERIC, and others—gave generously of their time and energy in discussing the issues. The National Council of Chief Academic Officers freely critiqued the ideas contained in this monograph and many of their suggestions are incorporated here. Reviewers for whose insightful comments and generous assistance we are particularly grateful are: Dr. Donald Grunewald, Former President and now Distinguished Professor, Mercy College; Dr. Reginald Wilson, Director of the Office of Minority Concerns of the American Council on Education; Dr. John Bennett, Director of the Office on Self Regulation Initiatives of the American Council on Education; Dr. John Andes; Professor of Education, West Virginia University and Dr. Milton Greenberg, Provost and Vice President for Academic Affairs at the American University, Washington, D.C. Dr. Walter S. Jones, Senior Vice-President for Academic Affairs and Provost at Wayne State University in Detroit, Michigan, made particularly cogent comments, the essence of which we incorporated into our introductory chapter. Finally, a network of researchers around the United States stimulated our thinking and consistently reminded us how complicated part-time faculty issues are. We acknowledge the help of these persons with gratitude and hope that the widespread exposure this manuscript has received will make it useful to a broad spectrum of readers if it contributes to a more rational approach to the management of academic part-timers, we will consider our task accomplished.

Our work is intended for campus administrators and personnel officials, faculty—relations committees, rank-and-tenure committees, department chairpersons, and others charged with hiring, nurturing, and evaluating part-time faculty. It will also be helpful to a variety of readers interested in a clear definition of the issues, a unified set of integrated policies, and a framework for orienting part-timers into the academic environment. It is our hope that the chapters that follow will help institutions to make effective decisions concerning how their part-time faculty should be treated.

PART-TIME FACULTY PERSONNEL MANAGEMENT POLICIES

——————— CHAPTER 1 ———————

Introduction

Policy Toward Part-Timers Is Relative

Although they were once a rarity on college campuses, over the last two decades part-time faculty members have become a growing and visible minority of the professoriate. While some disagreement exists on how part-time faculty should be defined, most researchers agree that part-timers are those who work less than a full-time load as this is defined by their employing institution. By this definition part-timers constitute better than one-third of those teaching in institutions of higher education (IHEs).[1] This represents a sizable increase from the early 1960s, and continued forecasts of declining student enrollments, restrictive federal aid policies, and tight budgets suggest that IHEs may employ even more part-timers over the next decade.[2]

The substantial growth in the number of part-timers has forced academic administrators to develop and implement personnel policies for this group. For the most part, these policies have been based on past practices. With the exception of the work of an American Association of University Professors (AAUP) committee, few formal documents have been available to provide a framework to guide institutions in integrating their part-timers into an academic work setting. Perhaps as a consequence, many academic administrators are uneasy concerning whether their part-time personnel policies meet their institutional needs. This unease is increased by the recognition that temporary policies followed when part-timers were a transitory minority may not be well suited to the changing academic setting.

An increasing number of administrators have also recognized that part-time faculty personnel management policies must differ from those governing other faculty. This reflects the unique role part-timers play in academe. Full-time faculty regularly submit to a relatively rigorous and codified set of standards for selection, tenure, promotion, salary review, and overall evaluation. In contrast, relatively few institutions subject part-timers to a formal review process. Since part-timers are rarely tenured, normally not involved in educational governance, and without day-to-day access to those who affect their status, the need for personnel policies that protect their rights, treat them fairly, and maintain their professional interest and stature is acute.

Such policies must reflect the need for accountability, responsibility, and compliance with the network of rules, expectations, and duties that define and order the academic environment. They must also balance the needs of institutions against the needs of their part-time employees. A major advantage the part-timer offers his or her institution is flexibility to meet enrollment swings, unexpected changes in demand for particular courses, or other last-minute developments. To deny an institution the flexibility to use its part-timers is to reduce its incentives for hiring this group. On the other hand, to deny the part-timer a degree of stability in employment and clear notice regarding the terms and conditions of his or her employment is to ignore the requirements for fairness and equity that this group deserves.

A similar issue exists with regard to what part-timers are paid. A policy of paying part-timers an amount equal to full-timers not only reduces the incentive to hire them but also raises several equity issues. Some institutions pay remarkably little to their part-timers, and this gives rise to claims that part-time faculty are "exploited." The issues surrounding what is fair payment are complex and we deal with them in some detail later in this book. For the moment, it is sufficient to point out that a well-defined set of policies must balance institutional needs for flexibility and human needs for clear role definition and fair treatment. The chapters that follow provide the foundation for a meaningful part-time handbook. Their goal is to provide a unified guide that can be used to orient part-timers and integrate them into the structure of their employing institutions.

A growing body of literature has evolved to address part-time faculty issues, and many of the matters discussed in these chapters have been explored by other researchers. At the conclusion of our book, a selected bibliography of part-time studies is presented for those interested in further reading. In scanning this bibliography the reader will soon discover that the various articles represent pieces of a single rather than several mosaics. For example, considerable research has been conducted on due process and the issues this creates in establishing a collective bargaining unit for part-timers. The studies in this area have been conducted by and large in isolation from each other and the larger body of literature on part-time. For this reason, they do not provide a common framework for how part-time faculty should be integrated within their employing institution, nor have they been used to shape institutional policies and procedures.

This book is designed to provide an integrated set of major personnel policies and practices for part-timers. It takes into account the needs of three principal groups: part-timers, full-timers, and administrators of IHEs. The framework it establishes is a general one that encompasses a range of employment issues and that balances the need of the employing institution for flexibility, order, and internal equity with the need of part-timers for structure, certainty, and equitable treatment relative to other employees. Four objectives govern our work:

To recommend consistent, rational, and reasonable personnel management policies for those institutions that employ part-time faculty.

To minimize institutional and personal costs caused by poor or nonexistent personnel management policies.

To recommend equitable personnel practices that recognize the constraints imposed by institutional charters; public, private, unionized, or nonunionized status; and other unique characteristics.

To identify and incorporate in our recommendations the sometimes divergent needs of the principal groups.

The academic personnel polices that are currently valid are likely to evolve as time progresses. Prevailing notions of academic freedom, faculty rights, and tenure for full-time faculty are not written in granite, nor is higher education immune to the competitive forces that are reshaping banking, health care, and a host of other contemporary institutions. Today's exemplars may well be tomorrow's dinosaurs unless they are kept in good repair. The recommendations made here are valid in the current context but must be periodically reviewed to reflect changing institutional and personal needs. For example, in our chapter on tenure for part-timers and in other chapters where part-time faculty practices are discussed, a full-time faculty model is assumed. There is, of course, no certainty that full-time faculty rights as we know them today will survive the next decade or so. The need for academic institutions to survive in the future may lead to new expectations regarding the rights and responsibilities of full-time faculty, and, if so, some of the models presented here may require restructuring.

With a surplus of Ph.D.'s, a serious chance that retirement age will disappear altogether, new demands for social equality in the marketplace, and a changing knowledge base in many academic disciplines—with all of these pressures on IHEs—the concept of tenure may be subject to serious challenge. The growth of the gypsy scholar, the non-tenure-track position, and the "permanent" part-time employee base all pose a serious challenge to the assumption of "business as usual."

Institutions slavishly following full-time faculty personnel policy models when establishing personnel policies for part-time faculty will impose serious limitations on their management flexibility. As a result, virtually all institutions create separate personnel policies and procedures for their part-time faculty personnel. This requires, on the one hand, creative and flexible management approaches to deal with the many unique characteristics and the multitude of substantive personnel issues associated with the employment of part-timers. Yet, on the other, institutions need to ensure that part-timers are not exploited. This is a delicate balancing act and is extremely difficult to achieve.

We strongly believe appropriate personnel policies can be devised to ameliorate whatever unfair advantage institutions might be taking of their part-timers—whether consciously, unconsciously, or through benign neglect. To provide a clearly articulated standard for "fairness" is a key objective of this book. The various suggested policies outlined in our subsequent chapters, we believe, are fair, workable, and appropriate for IHEs. They represent our serious and entirely objective attempt to formalize and codify part-time faculty personnel policies based upon current mores and practices.

Notes

1. Howard P. Tuckman, Jaime Caldwell, and William Vogler, "Part-Timers and the Academic Labor Market of the Eighties," in *Part-Time Faculty Series*, Washington, D.C.: AAUP, 1978, pp. 88–104.

Note that these authors impose several additional criteria to define part-timers, excluding, for example, persons who are also students in their own departments, full-time faculty in part-time positions, etc. Note also that some institutions use a different schema altogether to differentiate part-timers from full-timers. They assign their faculty into categories of full-time, fractional full-time, and part-time. The fractional full-timers, who generally carry a load more than half-time but less than full-time, can be represented by a bargaining agent and can receive prorated benefits based on whatever their fraction of employment is. Part-timers, however, receive only a stipend for teaching or research responsibilities.

2. Howard R. Bowen, and Jack H. Schuster, "Outlook for the Academic Profession," *Academe* (71) September-October, 1985, 9–15.

CHAPTER 2

Who Is a Part-Time Faculty Member?

Full-time faculty in higher education usually have the following rights and privileges:

An important voice in the selection, retention, and termination of academic colleagues

The right to determine the programs, courses, and course content to be taught in their department

The right to define their own roles in unsupervised teaching and research

Within limits, the right to determine their own workload, content, and hours of work

The right to regulate their activities through a code of ethics

Within limits, the right to judge their colleagues' professional productivity and rights to promotion and other rewards[1].

These rights dramatize the important and relatively well-defined governance role that full-timers have assumed at academic institutions. While examples can be found of IHEs that fail to grant specific rights to these faculty, or that grant them under limited conditions, the vast majority of full-timers hold these rights in common. Over the years, the criteria for selection, retention, and promotion of full-time faculty have been highly codified, and these are embodied both in faculty handbooks and in the traditions of academic institutions. Specific standards exist, either de facto or de jure, for most full-time faculty personnel actions. Institutional policies and practices generally involve peer and administrative reviews of full-time faculty teaching effectiveness, service to the institution, research, creative work, professional activities, grant work, community service, and service to students.[2]

In contrast, at many institutions the rights of part-timers are not well defined and few written materials are available to consult when misunderstandings arise. Institutions lack a tradition in dealing with part-timers, since in the past most of these employees have been transitional. The rights these people had were usually defined by the person who hired them, usually the division head or department chair; and when that person moved on, a new set of policies were applied. As a consequence, a person who accepted part-time employment had little idea of what his or her rights were or of what his or her employer expected. The situation was no better at the administrative level. In many colleges no common policy existed as to terms of employment, responsibilities, or methods of accountability. A consequence was that the institution exercised little control over the hiring of part-timers and assumed little responsibility for their problems.

Part of the reason for the shadowy treatment of part-timers was that they were assumed to be transitory. It made little sense to define the rights of a group that was employed only in the short term. What difference did it make if a part-timer was highly productive or relatively unproductive? Likewise, part-timers were a small and largely unseen minority who taught mostly the evening classes full-timers did not want or who filled in for faculty members on leave. Since their problems were invisible, there was little reason to worry about solving them. These considerations changed as the growing ranks of longer-term part-timers became more vocal, and as changing legal precedents made it increasingly clear that part-timers did have rights, which IHEs ignored at their peril. Ever so slowly, part-timers emerged from the shadows and demanded a clearer definition of their rights and the terms of their employment. With this emergence came a greater interest in defining the part-time population to delineate its rights and duties.

Two Definitions of Part-Time Faculty Members

The definition of who is a part-time faculty member is neither as simple as in the case of full-time faculty nor as precise. The following examples highlight the variety of situations found in academe:

In 4-year College A, departments hire limited numbers of part-timers to teach the specialized courses its full-time faculty either do not have the expertise or the time to teach. Term contract appointments occur either sporadically or on a continuous basis, but each chairperson hires part-time faculty on a one-semester teaching contract payable upon successful completion of the course. A probationary period is usually provided to determine the part-timer's teaching effectiveness.

Two-year College B hires part-timers to teach 40% of its courses. Budgetary constraints and low student enrollments have forced administrators to allocate 60% of their personnel budget to part-timers on a per-course basis. Without low-cost part-timers, extensive course reductions and some full-time faculty salary cuts would have been made.

University C has a large number of tenured full-time faculty approaching retirement age. It permits these senior faculty members to reduce their teaching loads by 50% with a pro-rata reduction in pay and benefits. These tenured full-time faculty members are considered part-time faculty with tenure.

College D has two tenured female faculty and one tenured male faculty who teach with 50% loads in order to allow them time to stay home and raise children. Each has teaching load, salary, benefits, and governance responsibilities prorated on a part-time basis.

Two-year College E hires part-time faculty to teach 100% of its courses. The only full-time personnel at this institution are administrators and a departmental chairperson for each discipline.

Four-year College F has a part-time faculty member who has taught at least one course per semester for over 15 years. He attends committee meetings, has served on curriculum development committees at various times, and also has developed new courses.

Two professors teach accounting at College G. Their two full-time appointments have been merged into one full-time tenure-track appointment so that they can spend more time in their tax accounting firm.

University H has an internationally renowned distinguished jurist who lectures in one comparative international law course per year. The university accorded this individual its highest full-time rank—university professor—even though he is part-time.

The above examples illustrate an important point that must be appreciated in dealing with part-timers. Part-timers differ in terms of their motivations for being part-time and, as a consequence, in what they expect from their employing institution. This makes it difficult to formulate a single policy that meets the needs of all of the part-timers employed at that institution. Likewise, the work that a part-timer will be hired to perform depends on the employing institution's need, and this in part determines the type of employment the institution should offer. The recognition of this dual source of need has given rise to the two major part-time taxonomies currently in the literature.

The first taxonomy is demographic in nature and is designed to classify part-timers according to their reason for becoming part-time. One of the authors developed these as part of a 1976 AAUP-sponsored national study involving nearly 10,000 part-time faculty members. The categories suggest that part-timers have substantially different employment situations (and expectations), and the numbers in parentheses are the percentages of total faculty in the study in each category.[3]

1. *The semi-retired:* Ex-full-time academics who scale down their activities to a part-time basis; ex-full-timers outside of academe who are semi-retired; semi-retired who have taught part-time during their entire career (2.8%)

2. *Students:* Employed as part-timers in institutions other than the one at which they hope to receive a degree (21.2%)

3. *Hopeful full-timers:* Those with no prior experience in academe who are working part-time to become full-time, and those with prior experience working part-time because they cannot find a full-time position (16.6%)

4. *Full-mooners:* Those who hold another job of 35 or more hours per week (27.6%)

5. *Part-mooners:* Those with two or more part-time jobs of less than 35 hours per week (13.6%)

6. *Homeworkers:* Those who work part-time primarily to care for children and other relatives (6.4%)

7. *Part-unknowners:* Those whose reasons for becoming part-time are unknown (11.8%).

Note that some part-timers have other jobs to rely on as either a primary or a secondary source of income. This is important because it bears on their ability to gain access to such items as social security, health, disability, and life insurance. For these persons, fringe benefits may be of little or no consequence, while those without other employment may define them to be of major importance. Unfortunately, many IHEs disregard their part-time employees' individual status and hence ignore an important source of potential dissatisfaction. We shall return to this point in later chapters.

The other major taxonomy widely cited in the literature classifies part-timers on the basis of their employment situation. Developed by Sheila Tobias while she was Assistant Provost at Wesleyan University in Middletown, Connecticut, this approach is useful in defining specific rights for part-timers based on their degree of attachment to their employing institutions.[4] Tobias employs the following categories:

1. *Moonlighters:* Persons who are employed in another job but who teach one course. They have no fringe benefits, no tenure or sabbatical accrual, no advisees or committee work, or a departmental vote.

2. *Twilighters:* Persons who are not otherwise employed, but whom the institution chooses not to give a regular part-time faculty position. They have no departmental vote but receive prorated fringe benefits and have longer contracts.

3. *Sunlighters:* Regular faculty appointments and like regular full-time faculty in every way except the amount of time they work. They receive prorated fringe benefits, committee assignments, and advisees and are eligible for tenure and sabbatical accrual. Their probation period is no longer than 17 semesters and they have an opportu-

nity to negotiate for full-time faculty status at a later time.

4. *Persons on occasional part-time leave:* Those whose regular full-time faculty appointment is retained and whose probationary period is extended proportionately. They may extend their part-time leave or return to full-time status at any time. This category of part-time faculty is not restricted to women who have small children, although the expectation is that such people will use it most.

Steering away from these descriptive models momentarily, there are also ill-defined psychic reasons for people to want to teach on a part-time basis. A few suggested here highlight the difficulties associated with defining just who a part-time faculty member really is. Some individuals are willing to teach simply to meet some deep-seated yearning to do it, whether for compensation or not. One of the authors hired a part-time faculty member—a high-level government attorney—whose motivation to teach consisted solely of saying "thank you" to the various institutions that provided him with financial and educational opportunities. Other part-timers seek a classroom outlet that allows them to perform in front of a group. Others, committed to their discipline, want the opportunity to teach it. Still others want to be challenged by young and inquiring minds. Some seek indirect economic benefits. The lawyer teaching law courses with the hidden agenda and secondary purpose of building a client base is a case in point. The politician who wants to use an academic institution as a basis for obtaining respectability and credibility is another example. Some politicians teach in order to obtain student campaign workers. The reasons part-timers teach can be as varied as one's imagination. Most defy easy categorization. Yet sufficient numbers of part-timers with ego-gratification rationales for teaching increase the supply of available part-timers and thereupon push down the compensation levels an institution needs to offer to attract them to the classroom.

Conclusions

An institution considering how it ought to deal with its part-timers would do well to begin with the two major classifications raised. Only after an institution has grappled with who its part-timers are, what their needs are, and what its needs are can it begin to formulate meaningful policies.

Notes

1. Logan Wilson, *American Academics,* New York: Oxford University Press, 1979, pp. 144–71.
2. For an example of a thorough and comprehensive faculty review program, see "Regis College Faculty Evaluation Criteria Standards Evidence, 1983," Regis College, Denver, Colorado.
3. Howard P. Tuckman, "Who Is Part-Time in Academe?" *AAUP Bulletin,* 64(December, 1978):305–15.
4. Harry Ross, "Policy Considerations for the Use of Part-Time Faculty in Public Community Colleges," Ed.D. dissertation, West Virginia University, 1982, pp. 25–26.

CHAPTER 3

Equal Employment Opportunity and Affirmative Action for Part-Time Faculty

Federal, state, and local equal employment opportunity laws shape the employment practices of academic institutions. Colleges and universities receiving federal support are required, among other things,

> not to discriminate against any employee or applicant for employment because of race, color, religion, sex or national origin. [The contractor] will take affirmative action to ensure that . . . employees are treated . . . without regard to their race, color, religion, sex or national origin. Such action shall include, but not be limited to the following:
>
>> Employment, upgrading, demotion, or transfer; recruitment or recruitment advertising; layoff or termination; rates of pay or other forms of compensation; and selection for training[1].

This affirmative action clause is both specific and enforceable to both full-time and part-time faculty personnel actions.

15

Nonetheless, off-the-record discussions reveal that the part-time faculty employment practices of many academic institutions do not rigorously follow these guidelines. In fact, examination of the employment practices of institutions reveals that hires of part-time faculty are usually based on a combination of availability, teaching competency, willingness to accept relatively low compensation for services rendered, institutional needs at the moment, and academic credentials. The hurdles in obtaining qualified part-timers are already steep enough in the opinion of many academic administrators to render affirmative action of secondary concern. Moreover, many argue that affirmative action should not be of primary concern when part-timers teach a one semester and/or one course offering on an irregular basis.

A recent study of the part-time hiring policies of institutions reveals that the following steps are almost always followed if hiring is under the supervision of a centralized personnel office.[2]

1. The adoption, *in principle,* of federal affirmative action regulations throughout the hiring process

2. A requirement for specific documents (applications, recommendations, transcripts) to be included in part-time faculty candidates' files

3. A requirement for interviews with at least two administrators (dean, department chairperson, etc.)

4. Review of recommendations by the chief academic officer who finalizes appointments by letter or contract.

In some institutions part-time hiring is decentralized at the department level rather than centralized. Since department chairpersons are more concerned with filling teaching slots than with careful record keeping, applicant flow data on part-time faculty are often not maintained. Such institutions usually have no centralized data repository on advertising sources, applicant files, selection criteria, measures of teaching success, or the relationship of these data to the selection of part-timers. For these institutions, an initial and crucial step is a clearly stated and well-articulated equal employment opportunity policy. Such a policy not only should be on the books but should actually guide the hires that take place at the department level. Although virtually all institutions have equal employment opportunity and affirmative action statements, many do not explicitly cover part-timers. It is suggested that such statements be *specifically* adapted to include part-timers. The following statements, provided as sample part-time faculty personnel fair employment practices, are suggested as useful part-time faculty policy statements:[3]

Sample Part-Time Faculty Fair Employment Practices Policy. The Institution Is an Equal Opportunity Employer

This institution is an equal opportunity employer and, as such, takes affirmative action to ensure that applicants for part-time faculty employment are treated in compliance with applicable laws and regulations governing equal employment opportunity and non-discrimination in employment on the basis of race, color, religion, national origin, handicap, age, sex, or status as a disabled or Vietnam-era veteran.

Affirmative Action and Nondiscrimination Concept

This institution is committed to the concept of affirmative action to accelerate the achievement of equal opportunity for minority groups, women, the handicapped and disabled, and Vietnam-era veterans and to ensure equal opportunity in all aspects of part-time faculty employment and all other personnel actions, including but not limited to compensation, benefits, promotions, selection for training, and terminations. Any person responsible for employment or promotion should ensure that these decisions are based solely on a part-time faculty member's qualifications for the requirements of the position he or she is being considered for.

Part-Time Faculty Recruiting

In all solicitations to placement agencies or professional societies, a statement must be made indicating that all qualified part-time faculty will receive fair and equitable consideration for employment. Since it is the responsibility of the [insert where hiring authority lies in the institution] to coordinate all help-wanted advertising, that office will see that suitable statements are included in the appropriate advertisements.

The advertisement will make no reference to sex or age.

Reports on Fair Employment Practices

The [insert here the appropriate term for the institution: personnel office, office of the dean, office of instructional services, etc.] is responsible for answering requests for reports concerning part-time faculty employment practices. Therefore, any contract from agencies or groups requesting such information or reports should be directed to that office.

Sample Policy for Affirmative Action in Employing Part-Time Faculty

It is the policy of this institution to provide equal opportunity in all terms and conditions of part-time faculty employment. The intent of this policy is to prohibit discrimination and to promote the full realization of equal employment opportunity through a continuing affirmative program in each administrative unit outlined in the institution's overall affirmative action plan. This policy of equal opportunity applies to, and must be an integral part of, every aspect of personnel policy and practice in the employment, development, and treatment of part-time faculty applicants and members at this institution.

Responsibility

The head of each administrative unit with authority to employ part-time faculty members shall be responsible for working with the institution's affirmative action office in implementing the requirements of the plan. It is the responsibility of each unit head to provide sufficient time and effort to administer the affirmative action program in a positive and effective manner; ensure that recruitment activities reach appropriate sources of part-time faculty job candidates; provide reasonable opportunities to part-time faculty members to enhance their skills so that they may perform at their abilities; and provide for a system within the unit for periodical evaluation of the effectiveness with which the affirmative action plan is being carried out. Compliance with the intent of institutional policy and its affirmative action plan shall be part of the acceptable standards of performance for all heads of administrative units employing part-time faculty members.

Leadership and Guidance

The affirmative action office, under the auspices of the institution's [president or chief administrative officer—whichever is applicable] and reporting to the provost of the institution, shall provide leadership and guidance to administrative units in their employment practices that affect part-time faculty applicants. The affirmative action office shall periodically review and evaluate administrative unit program operations, obtain such reports as deemed necessary, and report to the provost of the institution as appropriate on overall progress. The affirmative action office will consult from time to time with such individuals', groups, or organizations as may be of assistance in improving the institution's program and realizing the objectives of the affirmative action plan.

Resolution of Complaints

The institution shall provide for the prompt, fair, and impartial consideration of all complaints of discrimination in part-time employment. Each administrative unit shall encourage the resolution of part-time faculty member problems on an informal basis. Procedures for the consideration of complaints shall include at least one partial review within the administrative unit and shall provide for appeals.

Administrative Guidelines

The affirmative action office shall be responsible for preparing guidelines and instructions as necessary and appropriate to carry out the intent of the institutional policies for employment of part-time faculty.

Once these types of policy statements have been adopted, it is suggested that they be widely disseminated. The following steps for internal and external dissemination of an institution's equal employment opportunity and affirmative action policies are worth considering.

Checklist for Internal Dissemination of Policies

1. Include this checklist in the institution's equal employment opportunity and affirmative action policy manuals.

2. Periodically publicize the equal employment opportunity and affirmative action policies toward part-timers in the institution's newspaper, magazines, annual reports, catalogues and other media.

3. Conduct special meetings with administrative, management, and supervisory personnel to explain the intent of the equal employment opportunity and affirmative action policies and each unit's individual responsibility for their effective implementation.

4. Schedule special meetings with faculty and staff to discuss the policies and explain the responsibilities of individual units.

5. Discuss the policies thoroughly in both faculty and staff orientations.

6. Meet with union officials, if any, to inform them of the institution's equal employment opportunity and affirmative action policies toward part-timers and request their cooperation.

7. Include nondiscrimination clauses in all union agreements and review all contractual provisions to ensure that they are nondiscriminatory toward part-timers.

8. Use institutional publications to publish articles covering equal employment opportunity programs and to publicize the progress (e.g., promotions, merit increases, etc.) of minority part-time faculty.

9. Post equal employment opportunity and affirmative action policies on institutional bulletin boards.

10. When part-timers are shown in catalogues or brochures, minority and nonminority faculty of both sexes should be included.

Checklist for External Dissemination of Policy

1. Inform all teaching units verbally and in writing of institutional equal employment opportunity and affirmative action policies for the hiring of part-time faculty. Stipulate that they should actively recruit and refer minorities and women to part-time faculty positions.

2. Incorporate the equal employment opportunity and affirmative action policy statements in teaching contracts for part-time faculty.

3. Notify minority and women's organizations, community agencies, community leaders, secondary schools, and colleges of institutional equal employment opportunity and affirmative action policies.

4. Communicate to prospective part-time faculty the existence of the institution's equal employment opportunity and affirmative action program.

5. When part-timers are pictured in catalogues or brochures, show minorities and nonminorities of both sexes.

Although these steps may seem unduly repetitious and burdensome, institutions should recognize that if a compliance review is undertaken, the good-faith meeting of affirmative action hiring goals and timetables is *expected*. Good intentions do not count—only results. An institution is obliged to actively seek minority and female part-time faculty and record its efforts. Recruitment efforts for part-time faculty should be recorded as carefully as recruitment efforts for full-time faculty and staff.

A sample affirmative action recruitment report for part-time faculty is depicted below.[4] We suggest that institutions designing a recruitment report follow this type of model.

Affirmative Action Recruitment Report for Part-Time Members

1. Title of position:

2. College or administrative unit:

3. Contract type:

4. Equal Employment Opportunity–6 classification:
   (Note: The personnel office can provide these classifications.)

5. Was a written position description prepared for this part-time faculty position?
   If so, please attach it to this report.
   If not, please explain why not.

6. Was the announcement published?
   If yes, list the names of the publications and referral organizations.
   List the numbers of responses from each.

7. Were efforts made to determine the availability of qualified minorities, veterans, and handicapped persons for the position?
   If yes, please describe.
   If no, please explain why not.

8. How many applications (curriculum vitae) were received?
   List as follows:
   Minority (male and female)
   Women (except minority)
   Nonminority male
   Handicapped
   Veterans

9. How many applicants were considered beyond preliminary screening?
List as follows:
Minority (male and female)
Women (except minority)
Nonminority male
Handicapped
Veterans

10. Give the name—sex—race—ethnic group of each candidate interviewed but not selected for the part-time faculty position. Indicate the specific criteria by which the selected part-time faculty member was determined to be better qualified for the position than those persons interviewed but not selected.

11. Give name, sex, and race—ethnic group of the part-time faculty candidate selected.

12. Give the names of the search committee members.

13. Give the names of the approving officials.

14. Give the date of the approval.

15. Give the date of submission to the affirmative action office.

16. Give the date of approval by the affirmative action office.

In chapter 3 sample policy statements, checklists for internal and external dissemination of equal employment opportunity and affirmative action policies, and an equal employment opportunity feeder report needed for the personnel office to prepare its Equal Employment Opportunity–6 report have been suggested as being important to the management of part-time faculty. These documents are recommended to the reader for possible adoption.

Notes

1. See Executive Order 11246 and Office of Federal Contract Compliance Programs Revised Order No. 4 for amplification of a recommended affirmative action clause for federal contractors.

2. Harry A. Ross, "Policy Considerations for the Use of Part-Time Faculty in Public Community Colleges," Ed.D. dissertation, West Virginia University, 1982, p. 87.

3. The sample policy statements were adapted from Ray T. Fortunato and D. G. Waddell, *Personnel Administration in Higher Education,* San Francisco: Jossey-Bass, 1981, pp. 97–99.

4. *Ibid.,* pp. 101–2.

CHAPTER 4

Making Part-Time Faculty Appointments and Reappointments

Selection Criteria

Educational institutions traditionally hire three types of faculty:

1. Permanent—those faculty in full-time tenured positions

2. Probationary—those faculty in full-time tenure-track positions seeking tenured status

3. Temporary—those faculty hired for a defined duration and usually not eligible to become full-time or tenured employees

Most part-time faculty are classified as temporary employees, and a variety of titles are accorded to them depending upon institutional preferences, traditions, and needs. Part-time faculty as a group are often referred to as associate faculty, temporary faculty, community faculty, reserve faculty, supplemental faculty, and percentage instructors.[1] Individual titles include the following:

Part-time (instructor, assistant, or associate professor)

Part-time professor

Adjunct (instructor, assistant, or associate professor)

Lecturer

Affiliate lecturer

Professional lecturer

Senior lecturer

Visiting professor.

Part-time faculty are usually classified according to the ranks at their employing institutions. If full-time faculty have the titles of instructor and assistant, associate, and full professor, part-time faculty are sometimes given comparable classifications. However, a majority of part-timers are likely to be hired as instructors, adjuncts, or unclassifieds, irrespective of their field or demographic characteristics.[2] At 2-year colleges, most part-timers are hired to unranked positions. For present purposes, and to avoid having to work with the several alternative classification schemes, we use the terms *entry level, middle level,* and *senior level* to rank part-time faculty. The reader may either translate these terms into his or her own faculty ranking system or adopt our classification in a part-time faculty manual.

The purpose of adopting several classifications is to enable the institution to apply different selection and hiring criteria depending on the type of person it wishes to hire. Where only one set of hiring policies is needed, a multiple classification scheme is unnecessary. The following suggestions are made for institutions wishing to match their job requirements with selection and hiring criteria of varying degrees of rigor.

Selection Qualifications for Part-Time Faculty

ENTRY LEVEL:

To qualify for appointment to an entry-level part-time faculty position, a candidate should have academic *or* professional experience comparable with that required for appointment to the full-time rank of instructor. *Academically,* a candidate should have made substantial progress toward the doctorate, if a doctorate is considered customary in his or her discipline. *Experientially,* the candidate should have an employment history relevant to his or her teaching field and of sufficient duration to satisfy the requirements of the course(s) being taught.

MIDDLE LEVEL:

To qualify for appointment to a middle-level part-time faculty position, a candidate should have academic *or* professional experience comparable with appointment to the full-time rank of either assistant or associate professor. *Academically*, an appointee to this rank should hold the doctorate, if this is customary in his or her discipline. *Experientially*, relevant full-time responsibility and achievement should be shown. Additionally, a candidate should have demonstrated capability for professional growth in his or her field.

SENIOR LEVEL:

To qualify for appointment to a senior-level part-time faculty position, a candidate should have academic *or* professional experience comparable with that of a full-time rank of full professor. Additionally, the equivalent of 10 years of teaching experience should have been attained with commendable ratings from students and other persons who have had an opportunity to observe and evaluate teaching styles. *Academically*, a doctorate should have been earned, if this is customary within that person's discipline, and contributions to scholarship made by that person to his or her field. *Experientially*, a candidate must have relevant full-time professional responsibility, significant achievement, and impressive standing in his or her professional field.

Documentation Requirements

Documentation of the initial hiring process can be important if misunderstandings later arise over contract terms or in the event of a compliance review. To avoid problems in the future, it is useful to enumerate the documents that ought to be kept at the time a part-time appointment is made. Our list is based both on common practices with respect to full-timers and on the possible special situations that may arise in the employment of part-timers. It is designed to be illustrative rather than all-inclusive, and no doubt some readers may find considerations unique to their organizations that require additional documentation. Nonetheless, the items presented below provide a useful departure point for an administrative system:

1. A current resume or curriculum vitae is needed, which includes pertinent information on which to base both initial appointment and reappointment decisions, such as degrees received, teaching experience, teaching evaluations, and professional affiliations.

2. A policy statement concerning the hiring of nontraditional learning institution graduates is needed. Unaccredited institutions such as Walden University and accredited ones such as Nova University, University Without Walls, Pepperdine, Antioch, and other experientially based learning institutions that award advanced degrees have competent and distinguished graduates. The nontraditional nature of these academic programs needs to

be recognized and a determination made as to whether degrees from these schools are acceptable.

3. An endorsement should be included from the teaching unit administrator recommending the appointment. A specific statement in the endorsement should read that being appointed to the part-time faculty does not guarantee a teaching assignment nor provide compensation.

4. Student teaching evaluations should be included when available.

5. Publications, if any, in a field pertinent to the course subject matter should be collected and retained.

6 Valid academic transcripts from the colleges or universities the person attended should be kept.

Follow-up part-time appointments should involve the collection and retention of the above information. Each appointment and reappointment should be based on the above criteria, and the appointee should be prepared to defend his or her selection if such action becomes necessary. We also suggest that initial appointments and reappointments be made for a finite period of time, perhaps 2 years. At the end of this time, if a part-time faculty member has not taught any course, consideration might be given to canceling his or her appointment because of nonuse.

Length of Appointment

Many institutions view part-time faculty members strictly as temporary employees and hire them solely on an as-needed basis. This can prove legally troublesome if a part-time faculty member assumes that his or her reappointment will be *proforma.* An expectation of reappointment, whether justified or not, can lead to a situation where breach of implied contract suits could be filed. An institution's interests are best served if it

clearly specifies its contractual relationship with its part-time
faculty members in advance of hiring them. Accordingly, we
suggest a policy statement similar to the one following to clarify
an institution's position regarding part-time faculty appointments and reappointments:

> A member of the adjunct faculty of this institution is appointed for
> a period of up to 2 years. The appointment must be considered for
> official renewal at the completion of this appointment period.
> Renewal can occur only after an analysis of course load require-
> ments for the ensuing appointment period has been made, verifi-
> cation of satisfactory teaching evaluations has been completed, and
> a review of the part-time faculty member's academic and profes-
> sional progress over the previous appointment period has been un-
> dertaken. Where a decision is made to renew the part-time faculty
> member's contract, a formal contract must be renegotiated for the
> ensuing period with the faculty member. A part-time faculty
> member will be compensated only for sessions during which he or
> she had specified contractual duties and for which specific services
> have been rendered.

Probation

An institution should have evidence of the teaching abilities of
its part-time faculty if it is to do an effective job of selecting,
classifying, and rewarding its part-timers. Several means are
available for monitoring part-time teaching:

1. In institutions with large numbers of part-timers, a coor-
   dinator can be hired to work with them. One function of
   this person would be to attend classroom lectures of part-
   timers on an occasional basis.

2. Where arrangements can be made, a limited number of
   full-timers can be paid an honorarium to attend, and
   report on, the classes taught by part-timers once each se-

mester. Alternatively, departmental chairs can be asked to attend at least one lecture taught by part-timers each semester.

3. In institutions where student evaluations are an accepted part of the evaluation of full-timers, comparable evaluations can be made of classes taught by part-timers.

4. Each part-timer can be asked to give a lecture, presentation, or portion of a course to a knowledgeable administrator or faculty peer. His or her performance would be evaluated.

We recommend that no probationary period be used unless this is required by union agreements or institutional policies. The selection process for part-timers should be rigorous enough that they can reasonably be considered competent. The reasons for imposing professional hiring criteria have been spelled out by one of the authors elsewhere.[3] In those instances where part-time faculty do not perform at expected levels of ability, the institution should take immediate and forthright action to remove the person from the classroom, even if this means buying out his or her contract. Should several such actions be necessary, then the institution should seriously reconsider the procedures it uses to select part-timers.

Accruing Seniority

Students of the career progression of part-timers usually assume that seniority should be measured either by part-time years of experience with the same institution or by total years of experience in academe.[4] However, institutions vary considerably in how they treat the previous experience of part-timers, including whether they use these years to grant seniority. If an institution has no policy of according seniority status to part-time faculty, we suggest that serious attention be given to establishing one. In recent years, an increasing number of part-timers have developed attachments to their institutions, which extend beyond a single course or a single year. These persons often identify strongly with their employing institution and they assume its identity and values. Such persons are an important adjunct labor force that deserves recognition for its contribution and reward for its loyalty. With increasing frequency the courts have come to recognize the rights of this group, and it behooves academic institutions to distinguish between regular part-timers and those hired only on an occasional basis. Not only is this likely to reduce dissatisfaction among the regulars, but it is also likely to stimulate greater loyalty.

The following policy statement that recognizes both seniority and meritorious performance is suggested as a model. It can, of course, be adapted to meet an institution's unique needs.

The [campus authority designated to do this—usually the provost] authorizes initial placement of part-time faculty into the entry-, middle-, or senior-level ranks. Rank and salary are determined by giving credit for each year of past college teaching (either part- or full-time), and for other appropriate educational experience, and up to one-half year for each year of related experience. The general guidelines the [campus authority] uses for determining seniority and thereby rank and salary are as follow:

1. One year of full-time service teaching at the [university, college, or 2-year college, as appropriate] level is equivalent to 1 year of experience for rank and salary determination.

2. Eighteen semester hours of part-time faculty teaching experience are equivalent to 1 year of experience for rank and salary determination.

3. Each 2 years of related educational (elementary or secondary school teaching), industrial, or research experience may be equated to 1 year of experience for rank and salary determination purposes, depending upon the degree of relevance of the experience to the teaching assignment.

Access to a Full-Time Position

An important finding of the AAUP research studies is that a class of part-timers exists that is part-time solely because they cannot find a full-time position. People in this classification tend to be more dissatisfied with their position than others, more likely to feel underpaid, and more concerned with the lack of adequate fringe benefits. They are also the ones most likely to request access to a full-time position and to litigate when their needs are not met. Their presence makes it imperative that academic institutions clearly articulate their position with regard to providing access to full-time positions for part-timers. A clear statement of position reduces misunderstanding on the front end and reduces the chances of litigation at a later date. An institution can take at least four different positions regarding access to full-time faculty appointments. The position it selects determines the way it words the policy statement.

1. The institution imposes different criteria for the selection and hiring of part-timers than it employs for full-timers. Its expectation is that the former will serve purely as temporary employees to whom it feels no permanent obligation and from whom it requires no long-term attachment. Seniority in a part-time position has no effect on eligibility for, or priority in, access to a full-time job.

2. The institution imposes either similar or different criteria for the selection and hiring of part- and full-time faculty. A person hired as a part-timer is free to apply for a full-time position should one arise in his or her employing department. The suitability of that person for hire is based on the criteria for the position. Years of part-time teaching are not counted toward experience in teaching.

3. An institution imposes similar criteria for the selection and hiring of part- and full-time faculty. A part-timer can apply for a full-time position should one arise in his

or her employing department. That person is judged by the criteria for the position, and years spent in part-time teaching are prorated (as in the preceding discussion of seniority) in determining experience level. Prior experience in the department does not give the part-timer priority for the available full-time position.

4. An institution imposes similar criteria for the selection and hiring of part- and full-time faculty. A part-timer who has met his or her department's hiring criteria and performed satisfactorily during his or her years of employment is given priority when a full-time position becomes available in his or her department.

Conclusions

These policy statements for appointment are designed to avoid the problems most often created when the terms of hire are not spelled out in advance. While no universal statements are applicable to all institutions, the issues raised with regard to selection, seniority, documentation, accrual of seniority, and access to full-time appointments are important ones that need to be addressed. Explicit recognition of the criteria used in the appointment process as well as of the limits of institutional obligations can avoid future conflict and help the part-timer better to understand the policies and practices of his or her employing institution.

Notes

1. For further information about how part-time faculty are categorized in two-year institutions, see Harry A. Ross, "Policy Considerations for the Use of Part-Time Faculty in Public Community Colleges," Ed.D. dissertation, West Virginia University, 1982.
2. Howard P. Tuckman, "Who Is Part-Time in Academe?" *AAUP Bulletin*, 64(December 1978):305–15.

3. Howard P. Tuckman and Barbara H. Tuckman, "Who Are the Part-Timers and What Are Colleges Doing for Them?" *Part-Time Faculty in Colleges and Universities, 1981 Current Issues in Higher Education* Washington, D.C.: American Association for Higher Education, 1981.

4. Howard P. Tuckman, Jaime Caldwell, and William Vogler, "Part-Time Employment and Career Progression," in *Part-Time Faculty Series,* Washington, D.C.: AAUP, 1978, pp. 74–85.

———————— CHAPTER 5 ————————

Establishing an Effective Program for the Remuneration of Part-Time Faculty

Academic institutions lack not only a model of what a fringe benefits package for part-timers should look like but also a model for an appropriate remuneration scheme for part-timers. Many different approaches exist for paying part-timers, and an institution contemplating its own program will find no guidelines and limited written material to guide its deliberations. The purpose of this chapter is to help fill this vital gap in the literature.

A variety of compensation schemes are currently used to pay part-timers. For example, a national study conducted by one of the authors found that institutions pay their part-timers by many methods including per course, per credit or teaching hour, per student, and/or prorated according to what is paid a full-timer. Some institutions pay a flat amount irrespective of field, experience, type of degree held, or other personal credentials, while others employ some or all of the above variables in arriving at a payment scheme. Likewise, while some institutions provide a salary increment to part-timers according to the number of years they have taught at that institution, many others simply pay their part-timers the same amount year after year. In a majority of institutions, the remuneration scheme for part-timers differs from that for full-timers.[1]

The fact that part-timers are paid differently from their full-time counterparts is more than just a reflection of "past practice" or tradition for several reasons. First, part-timers are generally assigned duties different from those required of their full-time counterparts. For example, they most likely are not required to serve on governance committees, to engage in advising and counseling, or to help in student placement. Second, part-timers are generally not required to keep up with or to contribute to their fields in the same way that full-timers are. For example, many institutions do not require part-timers to engage in research, to publish, or to stay current in the literature of their field. Third, many part-timers have lesser credentials than their full-time counterparts. For example, part-timers are less likely to hold a Ph.D. or terminal degree or to have as much academic experience as their full-time peers.[2] Fourth, most (but not all) part-timers have primary responsibilities elsewhere. Hence, they may not be able to put forth as much effort into their teaching as their full-time peers. The primary motivation for seeking part-time work is to allow time for other activities. To the extent that the part-timer does devote less time to academic pursuits, an argument can be made that he or she is less valuable as a teacher.

While each of these arguments has merit, they can at best provide a partial explanation of the salary differential between the two groups of faculty. If credentials and/or experience are the primary source of difference, then it is difficult to explain why part-timers with equivalent credentials to those of full-timers are often paid a rate less than proportional to that of their full-time counterparts. Moreover, adjustment of part-time payments to reflect differentials in work activities and effort expended does not fully explain this situation. And none of the above arguments explains why many part-timers receive the same flat amount each year. Presumably, faculty productivity increases with years of experience, and this should hold true even if faculty teach a reduced load. That part-time salaries remain constant from one year to another despite a high rate of inflation cannot be explained by these arguments. The argument is even less convincing in the case of 2 year institutions where public service and publication are not significant determinants of salary levels and where part-timers are still paid less than proportionately to full-timers.[3] It seems clear that factors other than personal credentials and workload differences are important in explaining differential treatments of part-timers.

An important explanatory factor may be the existence of separate labor markets for full- and part-time faculty. On the demand side, institutions hire part-timers for different reasons than they do full-timers. Most part-timers are hired solely to teach, often for a limited period of time. Morever, the demand for part-timers is usually significantly less than that for full-timers. Since most institutions do not impose the same stringent hiring criteria in hiring part-timers as they do in hiring full-timers, they face a more abundant supply of the former than of the latter. A consequence is that part-timers can be hired at significantly lower salaries than full-timers.[4] In addition, some institutions factor into their budgetary projections the use of lower-paid part-timers. An institution's ability to pay total salary costs that exceed these projections therefore becomes an issue. Of course, to the extent that the hiring criteria proposed elsewhere in this book are adopted, the supply of competent part-timers is likely to be diminished and the cost of part-time faculty will be somewhat increased.

A related factor is that the labor supply of part-timers is likely to be a local one, while that for full-timers is more likely to be nationally drawn. Because academic institutions are better able to exercise monopoly hiring power in a local market, they may have greater success in holding part-time wages down than in holding full-time wages down.[5] A limited monopoly position and abundant supply of labor make it possible for an institution to offer a flat amount to part-timers irrespective of their productivity or to hold the amount paid to part-timers constant from one year to the next. Conversely, the tighter the supply of part-timers, or the greater the competition for available part-time labor, the higher the amount an academic institution will have to pay and the more important it will become to have a rational and fair compensation scheme.

When part-timers were a small and temporary part of the professoriate, it hardly mattered that institutions failed to base their payment on a well-thought-out compensation scheme. If one part-timer did not feel he or she was fairly paid, there was always another who could be hired. But the substantial growth in the number of part-timers, the growing attention to due process in the treatment of this group, and increasing evidence that part-timers are a permanent part of the academic scene have altered this situation. It makes sense for an academic institution to take a careful look at the way in which it remunerates its part-timers to ensure consistency with institutional goals and with its ideas regarding the role of part-timers. Such a look should begin with a clear statement of the goals of a remuneration program.

The Goals of an Effective Remuneration Program

The aim of any remuneration program, whether for part- or full-time faculty, is to attract, motivate, and retain qualified people. Most programs will seek to ensure well-qualified persons are hired, motivated to teach assigned courses in a professionally acceptable manner, and encouraged to remain part of the institution for as long as their services are needed and they are interested in teaching. Each institution will inevitably set forth its own unique goals for an effective part-time remuneration program consistent with its larger institutional goals, treatment of full-time faculty, and budgetary position. To aid in the process of goal identification, we have identified the following as worthy of careful consideration. A remuneration program should:

   1. Be attractive enough to ensure an adequate supply of qualified part-time faculty

2. Be designed to ensure that valued part-time faculty already on the payroll are encouraged to remain at that institution

3. Be based on a logical and equitable salary structure that reflects the value of part-time faculty to their employing institution both absolutely and relative to full-time faculty (e.g., if inflation adjustments are given for one group, they should also be given for the other)

4. Reflect the rates paid to part-time faculty by other institutions in the area

5. Provide rational criteria for the remuneration of part-timers that recognize meritorious behavior and that apply to all part-time faculty

6. Reflect movement through the ranks through promotion

7. Be fair, even handed, and nondiscriminatory toward particular groups of part-timers

8. Have sufficient flexibility to accommodate differences in part-time faculty member's skills and performance and to recognize differing market conditions

9. Be reasonably simple to implement and administer

10. Take a realistic view of, and reflect, institutional constraints.

Resolving "Fairness" Issues

Before discussing the design of a rational compensation scheme for part-timers, it is useful to raise several issues. First, a question exists as to whose criteria should be used to evaluate the "fairness" of a compensation system. Second, the issue arises as to whether fairness should be defined absolutely or relative to some reference group such as full-timers. If the former is selected, then an ancillary question arises as to what extent, if at all, the differential workloads of the two groups should be taken into account. If the latter is selected, then the issue arises as to whether the elements of a compensation package for part-timers should reflect the performance criteria laid out in the part-time faculty manual or be based on independent criteria.

It is our position that the appropriate standard for judging fairness should be based on an institutional context rather than a national yardstick. What is "fair" is best determined in terms of the needs, traditions, constraints, market conditions, and philosophy of each institution. This holds true whether the institution is dealing with promotion criteria, hiring decisions, fringe benefits programs, or compensation schemes. It makes little sense to impose a national standard on a local institution if the consequence is that part-timers are treated either better or worse than full-timers, or if adoption leads to such high costs that it results in a substantial reduction in part-time employment. There are simply too many diverse part-time situations for a uniform model to have applicability to all academic institutions.

There are two caveats that should be noted with respect to an institutionally based criterion of fairness. If such a system fails to compensate part-timers adequately for their contribution to the institution, it cannot reasonably be called fair no matter what the context. This is particularly true if such a system is discriminatory toward part-timers as a group. Likewise, a system that fails to allow for reasonable salary progression over time violates prevailing goals for a compensation system and cannot be judged to be fair. While there may be some years in which no raises are granted either to part- or to full-timers, a long-term history of flat payments to part-timers while full-timers experience salary progression violates reasonable standards for compensation. The second caveat is that compensation schemes that provide a flat amount to part-timers irrespective of their personal credentials, field, or productivity violate the goals for a reasonable and fair compensation scheme as set forth above. There is little justification for such a scheme in an institution that is striving for a satisfactory integration of its part-time faculty.

With regard to the question of whether fairness should be defined absolutely or relative to some reference group such as full-timers, many considerations must be addressed. If the goal of the institution is to integrate its part-timers, it makes sense for it to consider a relative approach. The standards set forth for promotion and tenure elsewhere in this book suggest ways that a relative compensation scheme can be designed. However, it will be difficult for an institution to measure the differential in such activities as advising or academic governance. Inevitably, a judgment must be made as to how this differential can be reflected in a fair differential in wages.

An example of how such a differential could be set follows: Suppose that an institution assigns a weight of 20% to the value of the nonteaching and research activities of full-timers. (Such a weight could be determined from faculty accountability reports based on the average time full-time faculty spend at each activity in a week.) If the average starting salary of a full-timer at the assistant professor rank is $14,000, this would imply a workload-adjusted starting salary for part-timers of $11,200 (80% of $14,000). The implicit assumption here is that the full-timer's time is of equal value in all uses. If a part-timer then taught one-third the hours of a full-timer in his or her field, he or she would receive $3,733 per course. Such proration could be made for each department and each rank, and this would form the basis for compensating part-time faculty. A procedure like this would be fair in the sense that it would provide a direct link from the salary of a full-timer to the payment a part-timer receives.

One problem with this approach is that an argument can be made for treating long-term part-timers more generously than temporaries and part-timers with heavy loads more like full-timers than those teaching a 3-hour load. (See Chapter 6 for further discussion of this point.) A way to handle this would be to give part-timers an increase in earnings each year based on the increase that full-timers receive. Thus, in an institution where the full-timers experienced an increase of 6% per year for 5 years, a long-term part-timer would earn significantly more than a part-timer just entering the system. Of course, such a system raises several questions. Does the increase apply only to the prorated portion of hours taught (e.g., a person who taught a one-third load would get a one-third increase, or 2%) or to the full base salary upon which proration took place? Likewise, how do you handle the salary of a part-timer who teaches only one out of two or more semesters? The question of whether to augment the base or whether to augment the prorated base should be settled internally. However, we tend to favor the former both for its administrative simplicity and because it tends to preserve a clear differential between part- and full-timers from one year to the next. It should be clear, however, that selection of the former option favors the light-loader, while selection of the latter favors the heavy-loader.

An institution that wishes to place additional weight on the proportion of time a part-timer spends teaching may wish to consider a compensation scheme that gives a higher per-course or credit hour payment to part-timers with heavier loads. For example, the part-timer in the preceding example might receive $3,733 for the first course, $3,900 for the second, and $4,100 for the third. The total earned for teaching three courses is still below that earned by a full-timer, but a person teaching a full load (in this case three courses) has a salary much closer to that of a full-timer than a person teaching one course. Such a system would be desirable in an institution with a heavy hopeful full-time contingent. These persons, who hold a part-time position primarily to gain entry to full-time teaching, are likely to be heavily reliant on their earnings from their part-time job and are also more likely to resemble full-timers in the effort they devote to teaching.

For institutions that choose to rely on absolute compensation systems, the major criteria for fairness are likely to be prevailing market wage, productivity, and personal credentials. At present, virtually no data exist on the wages that prevail for part-timers in national markets, and hence the primary market standard for payment is likely to be a local one. A good measure of fairness for an absolute compensation system is whether that system is uniform, evenhanded, and reflective of the duties and responsibilities part-timers are expected to carry out.

There are no guidelines for whether it is preferable to pay part-time faculty on a per-course, per-hour, per-student, or other basis. Some forms of payment are better suited to laboratory teaching, others to large class situations, and still others to the type of credit system used by an academic institution. Hence, it is not possible to render a single uniform judgment regarding which payment basis is most fair. Whichever of these is used, however, a rational method for differentiating among part-timers is required to provide a perception of fairness. A compensation scheme must be perceived as fair if it is to meet the goals addressed earlier.

Sources of Differentiation among Part-Time Faculty

Some academic administrators will scoff at the notion of applying wide-ranging goals in determining part-time faculty compensation; but such goals are already incorporated into salary decisions for part-time faculty, whether overtly or intuitively. Virtually all academic institutions take note of, if not make direct provision for, the following:

FACULTY CHARACTERISTICS

The qualifications of part-time faculty should be considered when making part-time faculty salary determinations. Persons with minimal qualifications and modest teaching backgrounds should be considered to be entry-level persons and treated accordingly. It makes sense to incorporate personal characteristics into a part-time faculty compensation scheme if the goal is to raise the quality of the part-time labor force closer to the level prevailing for full-timers.

LENGTH OF SERVICE

Most compensation schemes, whether in industry, government, or academe, allow for past experience in determining entry salary. It makes sense to take a part-time faculty member's length of service into account both in setting starting salary level and in subsequent compensation. While adjustments need to be made to prorate part-time teaching, this is not difficult to do. A system that provides extra compensation to experienced part-timers is more likely to attract experienced part-timers than one that pays a flat amount, even if the yearly increment to salary is fairly small. This is because an adjustment for length of service is part of the perception of a fair system.

ADJUSTMENT FOR ACADEMIC FIELD

The supply and demand conditions in academic labor markets differ significantly for the over 70 fields represented at academic institutions. Faculty in high-demand disciplines, such as computer science and accounting, will probably have to be attracted by a "premium." If academic institutions are to hire *quality* part-timers in these disciplines, they may have to accept the "judgment" of the market and to pay differential amounts depending on the field of the part-timer.

INCREMENTAL PAY FOR NONTEACHING ACTIVITIES

If an institution requires its part-time faculty members to be involved in nonteaching activities such as student advisement, curriculum planning, or institutional governance matters, then the amount paid to part-timers should be adjusted to reflect their additional workload.

DIFFERENTIAL FACULTY PRODUCTIVITY

Virtually all institutions would like to encourage faculty productivity and reward meritorious behavior. Such rewards should apply to both part- and full-timers if the system is to be perceived as fair. An effective compensation scheme will find ways to recognize and reward meritorious behavior by part-timers. In the absence of such recognition, part-timers have little incentive to pursue excellence in teaching or to stay current in their fields.

FORMAL STATEMENT OF THE RULES

Faculty react best when they are aware of the "rules of the game." An incentive system is effective only if it is clearly defined, formalized, and followed. Hence, an institution would be wise to articulate in a formal manner how it intends to establish part-timers' salaries and how it will differentiate among part-timers. The following address ways that salary differentials can be systematically accommodated.

Establishing the Part-Timer Compensation Program

To establish an effective part-time faculty salary structure, three distinct steps should be followed:

1. Determination of the basic salary grades

2. Addition to the salary structure of the basic elements selected from the items described above

3. Incorporation of detailed control features to ensure that the selected program will be implemented according to plan.

The basic salary grades used to pay part-timers should be consistent with the classifications for promotion discussed in Chapter 9. One approach would be to use the part-time faculty ranks of entry, middle, and senior level. Another is to use the full-time ranks of instructor, assistant professor, associate professor, and professor. Some institutions use unranked or ungraded positions for their part-time faculty positions, but we recommend against such a practice because it does not accommodate a crucial ingredient of a successful compensation program: clear differentiation among employees based on well-defined criteria. Typically, academic institutions use rank to differentiate among faculty based on qualifications, experience, education, and institutional needs. However, some institutions may assign faculty a higher rank in order to give them a higher salary, and others may assign a lower rank because they cannot pay more. In either event, the criteria for assignment to a pay grade should be consistent with those for assignment to a rank.

Addition to the salary structure of the basic elements selected from the items described above is the next major component in an effective part-time faculty salary program. One way to accommodate this is to ensure each part-time faculty level is positioned in a salary grade model on the basis of an assessment of the part-time position's external and internal value to the institution. An example of this methodology for an entry-level part-time faculty member being paid on a per-course basis might be as follows:

The institution might first examine the external academic market to see what seems to be the "going rate" for part-time faculty members in similar nearby institutions. This external criterion might then be matched against the resources academic institutions have available to pay part-time faculty and the other elements that differentiate faculty (e.g., field, need for a Ph.D., etc.). Once these factors are assessed, a standardized salary for teaching a specific course could be established. The institution would then pay each part-timer within a predetermined salary range to accommodate the factors selected from the preceding list.

Such a system might create fairly wide disparities among faculty at each rank. The extent of the variation and the overlap between ranks would be determined by the elements that the institution chooses to reward and by the funds available at its disposal.

In an absolute system, the amounts paid to part-timers would be treated as independent of those paid to full-timers and no attempt would be made to link the two compensation systems. Hence, the factors that the institution rewards need not be the same for the two groups. In a relative system, an attempt would be made to ensure that the rewards for the two types of faculty were similar. Ideally, a part-timer with the same characteristics as a full-timer, who has the same credentials, experience, and field, would then receive an amount proportionally the same as that received by a full-timer with the same duties and the same characteristics. In practice, the compensation schemes adopted by many institutions will have characteristics of both types of systems. But an attempt should be made to design the system in terms of one of the two approaches.

Finally, the defined maximums and minimums of salary ranges should be clearly established and promulgated, and policy statements concerning who is authorized to adjust salary levels should be set down. An audit should be conducted of the salary increases to ensure they are in conformance with institutional salary program policies. If a formal structural model is used, it is essential to ensure that *equal pay for equal work* policies are enforced. Faculty, irrespective of their personal characteristics such as race, age, national origin, religion, or sex, should all receive comparable pay if their teaching requirements are similar, efforts are the same, responsibilities are matched, and working conditions are similar. Another important consideration when employing a formal model is that no part-timer should be able to go beyond the maximum of his or her range unless he or she is promoted to the next level.

The third step in establishing an effective part-time faculty salary structure is to establish control features to monitor the structure's effectivenss. Probably the best indicator of whether a compensation program is effective is how well it meets its goals. At the outset of this chapter, we stated that the goals of any compensation scheme are to attract, motivate, and retain qualified part-time faculty to teach in an institution. Monitoring a program's effectiveness is a matter of analyzing whether these goals have been achieved to the satisfaction of the academic institution. If effective teachers have been attracted, motivated to do an effective job, and retained, it is logical to assume the program is working effectively. When monitoring a salary program for part-timers, institutions should be sensitive to specific issues that may reduce effectiveness. Some of these issues are the following:

1. *Pay compression:* As newer part-time faculty members are hired by an academic institution, it becomes imperative their salaries not be unduly out of line with those prevailing there. Distortions due to differential operations of internal and external labor markets could cause new part-timers to be paid at a different rate than long-service part-timers brought in at lower salary rates in earlier years. If part-timers are paid on a prorata basis or on the basis of years of experience, this problem may not surface. However, if part-time faculty members are paid differing rates based on their hire date, this can become a significant problem that will reduce the effectiveness of the program.

2. *Grade distortion:* Some organizations attempt to circumvent a rigid part-time faculty ranking and compensation system by offering to promote part-timers as a means to increase their pay. This obviously is anathema to maintaining the integrity of a viable part-time faculty system of promotion based upon qualifications. One monitoring device to see whether this is occurring in an institution is to track whether numbers of entry, middle, and senior levels are distorted toward the upper ranks, either by department or for the institution as a whole. If this is occurring, it is likely that there are too many part-timers being promoted simply to provide more equitable compensation, and a review of the structure is in order.

3. *Satisfaction indexes:* An academic institution can determine whether its part-time faculty are satisfied with their relationship with the institution based on a variety of factors. Number of grievances filed, turnover rates, difficulty in recruitment of qualified people, teaching evaluations

provided by students, and general feedback from full-time faculty, other part-timers, and students are indicators that some aspects of the employment relationship are wanting. When this is the case, an institution would be wise to analyze whether the wage and salary structure is an important source of dissatisfaction for its part-timers.

Conclusions

The discussion in this chapter suggests that an effective part-time faculty remuneration scheme can be developed if an institution proceeds from a careful statement of goals. Based on these goals, a set of equity criteria can be evolved to deal with the joint issues of how fairness is measured in absolute or relative terms. The several items that differentiate full-time faculty need to be considered in the part-time context, and careful consideration should be given to personal credentials, field, and workload as factors affecting part-time earnings.

It is important to note that every institution will need to face the issue of a part-timer whose service, background, and teaching abilities are acceptable but not meritorious. In this instance, a mechanistic and reasonably scientific approach to salary setting may appear not to be in the best interests of the institution. Rather, an arbitrarily set stipend differentiating this faculty member from others may seem desirable. We disagree with any notion of arbitrarily setting salaries for part-timers without clearly defining equity criteria. A salary system without well-defined performance criteria invites both chaos and inequity. Therefore, we believe a defined merit component should be built into any part-time faculty salary system to recognize any exceptional service, high qualifications, quality of publications, quality of credentials, university service, and effective teaching. This notion does not do violence to logically defined and mechanistically derived salary ranges as we have described in this chapter. A carefully thought-out merit component differentiates individual part-timer backgrounds and contributions as well as recognizes part-time faculty members who are performing above institutional expectations.

The remuneration scheme chosen should be one with defined limits and formal rules, and it should lend itself to audit and to monitoring. It should also reflect the duties and responsibilities for part-timers laid down elsewhere in this book.

Notes

1. Howard Tuckman and Jaime Caldwell, "The Reward Structure for Part-Timers in Academe," *Journal of Higher Education,* 50 (November-December 1979): 745-760. See also Barbara H. Tuckman and Howard Tuckman, "The Labor Market for Part-Time Faculty at Business Schools," *Quarterly Review of Economics and Business: Journal of the Midwest Economics Association,* 24 (Autumn 1984): 95-103.
2. Howard Tuckman, "Credentials, Educational Quality, and the Role of Part-Timers," *Change,* (January-February 1981): 8-10.
3. Howard Tuckman and William Vogler, "The 'Part' in Part-Time Wages," *AAUP Bulletin,* (Summer 1978): 70-77.
4. *Ibid.*
5. Howard Tuckman, *Publication, Teaching, and the Academic Reward Structure,* New York: Lexington Press, 1976.

CHAPTER 6

Part-Time Faculty Benefits Administration

Neither tradition, common practice, nor professional association recommendations have established a set of guidelines that institutions can use in deciding what is an adequate fringe benefits package for academic part-timers. Instead, a patchwork of different coverage arrangements exists, based more on happenstance than on conscious choice. Depending on the institution at which they are employed, part-timers may find themselves covered by one or more of the following packages:

No fringe coverage at all

Social security

Social security plus partial private retirement

Social security plus partial life insurance

Social security, partial retirement, and partial life insurance

In rare cases, social security, partial retirement, and life, sick leave, and/or health insurance

53

Additional fringes such as parking, subsidized meals, library use, etc.

It is difficult to predict the type of coverage, if any, a given academic institution will provide. Institutions generous in the fringe benefits they provide full-timers may offer little or no benefits to part-timers. Likewise, institutions with a large proportion of part-timers do not necessarily provide extensive fringe benefits to this group. Given these circumstances, a part-timer entering an institution for the first time is likely to have little idea of what to expect in the way of fringe benefits offerings. This makes it imperative that an institution wishing to orient its part-time faculty state its fringe benefits policies clearly in its part-time faculty handbook.

One rule of thumb seems to hold fairly universal: The greater a part-time faculty member's teaching workload, the more likely that person is to receive fringe benefits coverage. The importance of the relationship between workload and coverage was highlighted in a study of academic institutions conducted by one of the authors several years ago.[1] Table 6.1 reproduces his findings. Note that in all fringe categories institutions are more likely to provide coverage to those employed

TABLE 6.1

Percentage of Part-Time Faculty Who Receive Fringe Benefits from Teaching by Workload and Type of Benefit

	PART-TIMER'S WORKLOAD		
	Less than half-time	More than half-time	Combined
Social security	44	59	47
Retirement plans	15	37	19
Sick leave	11	22	14
Medical insurance	5	21	8
Workers compensation	10	19	11
Life insurance	4	16	6

*Rounded to nearest whole number.

with half the load of a full-timer or more (the heavy-loaders) than to those employed less than half-time (the light-loaders). Note that with the exception of social security few institutions provide much fringe benefits coverage for their part-time faculty.

General Benefits Considerations

Federal, state, and local government statutes require that employees be covered by certain fringe benefits programs. These programs are social security, workers' compensation, and unemployment insurance. Federal law specifies employer–employee contribution requirements as well as payout levels for social security. State statutes establish eligibility requirements for workers' compensation and unemployment insurance, with the tax rates on employers, terms, and coverage determined at the state level. However, with respect to benefits beyond those legally mandated, academic institutions have the latitude to create and offer any type of benefits programs they wish and to decide who should be eligible for coverage. This right is somewhat limited in public and unionized organizations where benefits programs are either legislatively dictated or negotiated. Nonetheless, an institution has the right to provide a benefits package to its employees based on its own philosophy concerning the role of fringe programs in academe. This includes the right to provide few or even no benefits other than those prescribed by law. The choice of benefits offerings— magnanimous or meager—will reflect an institution's philosophy, financial status, and past practices.

The primary reason for establishing a fringe benefits program is to provide noncash compensation competitive enough to attract, motivate, and retain employees. Fringe benefits protection may also be provided for reasons of equity, to protect employees from random events that impose severe costs on them, or as a form of remuneration in place of cash. In determining whether fringe benefits should be provided to part-timers, the following factors are likely to be considered:

- Cost Factors
  - Is a fringe package less costly than cash payments?
  - Are there tax advantages in using fringe packages?
  - Can group discounts provide fringe benefits more cheaply than employees can receive them elsewhere?
  - Do fringe benefits costs grow less rapidly than salary costs when inflation increases?
- Productivity Factors
  - Can fringe payments attract hard-to-get employees?
  - Can fringe benefits increase productivity, loyalty, and/or institutional attachment?
  - Can part-time coverage be integrated into existing full-time plans?
  - Do competitive institutions offer fringe packages?
- Equity Factors
  - What is the obligation of the institution to those without fringe benefits coverage (e.g., full-mooners are likely to have coverage elsewhere, while hopeful full-timers usually have no coverage except what they receive from their employing institution)?
  - What is the obligation of the institution to its long-term employees?

Once a decision is made to cover part-time employees, if it is made, a wide variety of noncash benefits are available for possible adoption. Any or all of the following are worth serious consideration. These potential fringe benefits are comprehensive in scope. Their being listed does not, however, constitute our recommending they be provided to part-time faculty.

Potential Fringe Benefits

PENSION PLANS

Any part-time employee working 1,000 hours or more during a 12-month period can count that year toward pension eligibility under the provisions of the Employee Retirement Income Security Act of 1974, as amended. Since a majority of part-time faculty members do not work 1,000 hours during a year, they are not usually considered pension eligible. However, an institution can decide it wishes to include part-time faculty in an employee pension plan on a prorated basis based on hours worked. That institution must first decide who is eligible for pension plan membership. More liberal exceptions to this minimum standard are permissible.

If an institution's pension plan is a *defined contribution plan* (sometimes referred to as an *individual account plan*), the institution pays a predetermined amount into its pension fund for each pension plan member. A pension plan-eligible part-time faculty member can also contribute depending upon whether the plan is contributory or noncontributory. All payments into the pension plan accumulate, along with investment and interest earnings, in separate pension plan participant accounts. The employee's retirement benefit is determined by the total dollar amount in his or her account at retirement. It is therefore impossible to predict an actual retirement benefit level until retirement.

If an institution's pension plan is a *defined benefit plan,* the employee's retirement benefit is predetermined in advance. The retirement benefit is linked to the employee's earnings, length of service, or both. Three types of benefit formulas can be used to determine how much a part-time faculty member will receive upon retirement if an institution decides to permit part-time faculty to be pension plan participants:

1. A *flat benefit* formula pays a specific dollar amount per year of service. This approach is common among unionized employers.

2. A *career-average* formula averages the pension plan member's yearly earnings over his or her part-time faculty teaching career. The dollar value of the pension received is a percentage of the career average. This approach is common among nonunionized employers.

3. A *final-pay* formula bases benefits on average earnings

during a specified number of years at the end of the part-time faculty member's teaching career. Retirement benefits equal a percentage of that employee's final average earnings multiplied by his or her years of part-time service. This is the most common formula found among nonunionized, salaried employees.

THRIFT PLAN

Thrift plans, also known as *savings* and *investment–savings plans*, are defined contribution plans. Thrift plans generally require a full- or part-time faculty member to contribute part of his or her teaching income to the academic institution. Typically, an institution will match completely or in part the faculty member's contribution. These contributions are placed in a trust fund and invested in an investment income-producing instrument (e.g., fixed-income bonds). Riskier investments such as stocks and real estate can also be used as an investment vehicle. For record-keeping purposes, each thrift plan participant's savings and investment earnings are assigned to his or her individual account.

A typical plan allows a full-time or part-time employee who is at least 21 years of age and has 1 year of service to participate.

A large majority of thrift plans are contributory in nature. These involve one of two arrangements: (1) *basic contributions,* which are fully or partially matched by the employer, or (2) *supplemental contributions,* which are employee contributions not matched by the employer.

An employee's contribution can be made from after-tax income or through some type of salary reduction plan. In the private sector, salary reduction plans are fairly common. These are commonly referred to as 401(k) plans after paragraph 401(k) of the Internal Revenue Code (IRC) of 1954.[2] Nonprofit organizations and educational institutions are also eligible to participate in salary reduction plans. These plans are referred to as tax-sheltered annuities (TSAs), or 403(b) plans [named after section 403(b) of the IRC].[3] When offered by an institution, a TSA permits a full- or part-time faculty member to exclude from his or her gross income contributions to the plan. The ensuing savings are intended for retirement but can also be used, without penalty, for emergencies, loans, or a source of income in the event of disability or death. Employer contributions and investment earnings on employee–employer contributions to TSAs are not taxed as ordinary employee income until they are actually received.

HEALTH INSURANCE

Virtually all academic institutions provide health insurance to their full-time employees, but few offer it as a fringe benefit to part-timers. An academic institution can offer its employees two generic types of health plans: (1) prepaid plans, such as those offered by health maintenance organizations (HMOs), and (2) postpaid plans, which are plans offered through an insurance carrier. HMOs emphasize preventive treatment and early diagnosis of illness. They provide basic comprehensive physician services, outpatient services, instructions on procedures to be followed to secure emergency health services, drug abuse treatment and referral services, diagnostic laboratory and diagnostic–therapeutic radiologic services, home health services, and certain preventive health services for a fixed monthly prepaid premium. These services are usually administered from a centralized health care delivery location. Supplemental HMO services can include facilities for intermediate- and long-term care, vision and hearing care, dental services, mental health services, long-term physical medicine and rehabilitative services, prescription drugs, etc. Care is available around the clock. Under the HMO Act of 1973, all employers with more then 25 employees are now obligated to offer them the option of joining a federally qualified HMO when medical fringe benefits are offered.[4]

Postpaid plans are categorized as *basic medical* and *major med-*

ical insurance plans. Medical benefits are provided through basic and major medical plans in three ways:

1. *Service Plans:* All *usual, customary,* and *reasonable* (UCR) costs for medical care are paid in full by a medical insurance carrier. If the designated carrier pays all UCR costs and the provider of the medical care accepts UCR payments as payment in full, the employee pays nothing more for his or her medical care. *Fee for service*-oriented medical plans are more often found as a "fringe" benefit than either of the two plans mentioned below.

2. *Indemnity plans:* Indemnity plans are also referred to as *scheduled plans* because they pay specific scheduled amounts for covered illnesses and treatments. For example, an indemnity plan would pay a fixed amount for hospital room and board for a scheduled number of days. Any amount that exceeds the scheduled amount must be paid by the employee, another insurance carrier covering the employee, or possibly a major medical plan.

3. *Combination plans:* This type of medical plan provides both service and indemnity coverage. An example would be a plan paying UCR amounts for hospital room and board plus a scheduled amount for a specific medical treatment. Certain characteristics of medical plans need to be clarified. The *deductible* refers to the amount a plan participant pays out of his or her after-tax dollars *prior* to receiving reimbursement for medical expenses. The *maximum limit* defines the maximum limit of monthly, annual, or lifetime coverage a carrier will assume. Most major medical policies have a maximum limit on what they will pay. *Coinsurance* involves the residual amount that the participant pays before the carrier pays the remainder. For example, if a plan calls for the carrier to pay 80% of all UCR medical expenses after the employee pays the deductible, then the employee is obligated to pay 20% of incurred medical expenses. Some plans have a coinsurance *maximum* where the carrier pays 100% after the

employee pays a certain dollar amount out of pocket, for example, $2,000.

DENTAL CARE

Dental insurance is a fringe benefit found, as of 1983, in some 92% of private-sector firms.[5] Generally, dental insurance (1) covers many dental care costs and (2) encourages employees to seek preventive dental attention, thereby detecting and preventing possible serious dental problems. Typical dental plans include the following features:

1. Diagnostic procedures

2. Preventive procedures such as cleaning, scaling, and fluoride treatments

3. Restorative procedures such as repairing teeth and providing fillings and other crown work

4. Oral surgery

5. Endodontics (treatment of teeth with diseased roots)

6. Periodontics (treatment of gum diseases)

7. Prosthodontics (replacement of missing teeth with fixed or removable prostheses)

8. Orthodontics (correcting malpositioned teeth)

There are typically four types of dental plans:

1. *Nonscheduled plans:* These plans cover UCR charges for employee dental work.

2. *Scheduled plans:* The schedules involve a flat dollar amount to be paid for each dental service performed.

3. *Combination plans:* These plans combine a UCR plan with a schedule of benefits.

4. *Closed-panel plans:* This is essentially an HMO for dental problems. Employees go to a designated panel of dentists who provide specific treatment in accordance with a previously arranged relationship with the employer and in conformance with premiums paid.

PRESCRIPTION DRUG PLANS

Prescription drug plans are relatively new as an employee "fringe" benefit. They have been offered in the private sector for about two decades and provide insurance coverage for out-of-hospital prescription drugs. The most common types of plans include the following:

1. *Open-panel plans:* These plans permit employees to go to the pharmacy of their choice to have prescriptions filled.

2. *Closed-panel plans:* Plan-associated pharmacies dispense drugs to plan members at prices prearranged by both the plan carrier and the pharmacies.

3. *Mail-order plans:* Employees send in prescription orders directly to a centralized pharmaceutical mail order location.

4. *Nation-wide panel plans:* Through the use of a nation-wide network of pharmacies, employees obtain prescriptions directly from participating pharmacies, paying with a specially issued credit card.

GROUP LIFE INSURANCE PLANS

Group life insurance plans are designed to provide death benefits for survivors of deceased employees. They are typically annually renewable term insurance plans. A common group plan is one that represents a flat percentage of an employee's salary. For example, the face value of a group term policy may be expressed as 130% of an employee's salary, recalculated annually. The employer either pays the full amount of the premium, shares the cost of the premium with the employee, or has the employee pay the full amount, depending on the terms of the plan. Often, accidental death and dismemberment is a major feature of group term insurance. This coverage usually pays a multiple indemnity for death by accident, and in the case of accidental dismemberment pays specifically scheduled benefits to a policyholder. A typical group term plan permits an employee to convert his or her term coverage to a whole-life policy without proof of insurability in the event of employment termination or retirement. Group life insurance plans are an important and widely desired fringe benefit.

DISABILITY INCOME PLANS

Private disability income plans, when coupled with legally required state worker's compensation plans, can restore a measure of income and dignity to a disabled employee until he or she regains earning powers. Typical plans are categorized as short-term or long-term disability plans. *Short-term disability* is defined as the inability of an employee to perform normal occupational duties. Short-term disability plans typically range anywhere from 13 weeks to about 24 months of coverage. Generally, they replace in the neighborhood of 50—75% of an employee's predisability gross income, calculated on a weekly basis.

A *long-term disability* is defined differently. Long-term disability means an employee is unable to perform any job that he or she can be reasonably expected to perform on the basis of training, education, and experience. After short-term disability benefits have expired, and the employee is considered to be long-term disabled, long-term disability benefits will be triggered based on the terms of the policy. Disability income payments range from about 75 to 80% of a disabled employee's predisability pay.

Often disability income plans will include a statement that an employee's integrated total disability income from public and private sources cannot exceed a certain percentage of predisability gross pay. Long-term disability payments may be offered to disabled employees for a finite period of time such as 10 years, or more often until other benefits are activated, such as social security and private retirement benefits. Some plans also permit long-term disability payments to be paid with other retirement benefits.

SICK LEAVE

Most academic institutions have sick leave policies that allow employees a certain number of sick leave days each year. The number of days taken can vary greatly depending on whether a plan is *annual* (i.e., specifies an authorized number of paid sick leave days per year) or *per disability* (specifies the number of days available for each absence stemming from an illness or injury). Length of service is often relevant in calculating the paid sick leave days for which an employee is eligible.

Academic institutional policies for faculty sick leave generally follow no standard pattern. Some provide for no faculty sick leave at all, requiring an ill or injured faculty member to arrange for his or her own substitute in the classroom. Other institutions have annual or per-disability sick leave polices similar to those found in the private sector. Private-sector sick leave policies typically address the issues of accumulation of unused sick leave from one year to the next and coordinate sick leave with health insurance coverage.

Institutions wanting to consider offering paid sick leave days to its part-time faculty would be wise to consider adopting an inclusive sick leave policy that addresses these two issues. A policy that might be considered would include permitting a part-time faculty member who teaches, for example, 3 contact hours per semester to accumulate 3 hours of paid sick leave per semester.

LEGAL SERVICES PLANS

Legal services plans, also referred to as *prepaid legal services* and *group legal services plans*, are not taxable to employees as gross income in accordance with the 1976 Tax Reform Act. Legal services plans offer employees reduced legal rates as well as protection against lawsuits. Additionally, they offer a form of preventive legal advice that reduces an employee's risk of being legally vulnerable to every day exigencies. Typically, legal services plans are prepaid.

Legal services plans can be characterized by four distinct features:

1. *Consultation:* An employee can seek consultative services concerning matters such as consumer and landlord–tenant disputes and domestic issues. These can be offered in an attorney's office or over the telephone. Consultation is a commonly found feature of most legal services plans.

2. *General nonadversarial work:* This feature permits a variety of legal services such as name changes, drawing a will, creation of trusteeships, etc., to be performed in an attorney's office. Because of its relatively low cost, general nonadversarial work is commonly found in most legal services plans.

3. *Domestic relations:* This is an exceptionally expensive service. It covers separations, divorces, child custody issues, and like items. Because of the expense involved, few legal services plans include domestic relations as part of their coverage.

4. *Trial and criminal work:* The high expenses associated with this coverage cause most legal services plans to exclude trial and criminal work. Civil suits, minor criminal issues, midemeanors, and the like are covered if this feature is part of a legal services plan.

VISION CARE

Traditional health insurance plans have provided little or no vision care coverage as an employee fringe benefit. A typical vision care plan covers eye examinations, lens prescriptions, frame selection, and frame fitting. Virtually all such plans impose specific limitations on the frequency of covered services and on the dispensing of glasses. These limitations generally include one eye examination per year and one set of lenses per year.

LIBRARY PRIVILEGES

A number of academic institutions do not provide library privileges to any of their part-time employees. Such policies can adversely affect a part-time faculty member who needs to remain current in his or her academic discipline through the study of written materials. The provision to part-time faculty members of library cards, access to library stacks, and book check-out privileges enhances both their professional capability and their sense of belonging to their academic institution at a small cost to the institution.

PARKING PRIVILEGES

A seemingly trivial but often important fringe benefit centers on part-time faculty parking assignments. If, for example, a part-time faculty member is teaching one course per semester, it is unfair to expect that person to pay the same parking fees as a full-timer who parks on campus every day. An equitable policy that either assigns parking spaces or reimburses part-time faculty members for parking costs on a use basis is a low-cost but positive way of attracting, motivating, and retaining part-timers.

SABBATICAL ACCRUAL

Rarely do academic institutions offer part-time members an opportunity to accrue time, even on a prorated basis, toward a sabbatical from teaching obligations. Typically, if a part-time faculty member wishes to take time off from teaching, it is common practice simply to contract for another qualified person to assume his or her teaching obligations. Paid sabbaticals are usually not available to part-timers to improve their academic skills, and an issue exists as to whether they are warranted. However, if an institution wants to provide part-time faculty with sabbatical leave, a policy could be established, making accrual on the same basis as for full-time faculty. Such accrual could be determined on a prorated basis—as a percentage of the workload of a full-time faculty member.

EDUCATIONAL BENEFITS

A number of academic institutions permit full-time faculty, staff, and their spouses and children to enroll in courses either free of charge or at a reduced rate. This benefit is a perquisite widely prized by institutional employees, their families, and members of families of deceased or disabled employees. Rarely are such tuition remission benefits available to part-time faculty members. If an institution believes it appropriate to provide education benefits to part-time faculty, these could be offered on a prorated basis.

GRANTS IN SUPPORT OF SCHOLARSHIP

Many academic institutions offer their full-time faculty grants in support of scholarship. These grants are typically not-accorded to part-time faculty. If an institution wishes to award scholarship grants to attract, motivate, retain, or reward part-time faculty, then a policy could be established whereby part-time faculty would be able to receive grants in support of scholarship on the same basis as grants are offered to full-time faculty. This might mean either prorating as a percentage of the workload of a full-time faculty member, offering grants equally, or making them available to all faculty based on competitive criteria.

CAFETERIA BENEFITS OR FLEXIBLE BENEFITS PLANS

No description of employee benefits would be complete without at least passing reference to what are called *cafeteria benefits* or *flexible benefits plans*. The IRC, section 125 (d), defines a cafeteria benefit plan as "a written plan under which (a) all participants are employees, and (b) the participants may choose among two or more benefits." Typically, employees are given a standardized package of benefits irrespective of their personal situation. This can lead to redundancy of benefits in some instances or to a surfeit of benefits in others. For example, a young, married professional may be far more interested in medical benefits for his or her family than in retirement benefits. Likewise, an older employee whose spouse also works and is covered by an employer's medical plan probably does not need double medical coverage, but would like to see benefits accumulating toward retirement.

To be responsive to differing employee wants, increasing numbers of employers are adopting a cafeteria benefits plan selection approach. Typically, a floor of core benefits is established that ensures an employee receives basic coverage. Beyond this core, an employee chooses among a smorgasbord of predetermined benefits plans based on his or her wishes and life-style. The chosen benefits may be nontaxable or taxable and may take the form of cash, property, or others. Cafeteria benefits plans are difficult to administer and can create personal and financial hardships for employees who select what turn out to be the wrong benefits. Furthermore, the Internal Revenue Service has been inconsistent in its tax treatments of benefits. In 1984, for example, it found that zero-balance reimbursement accounts (so-called zebra accounts) were considered taxable income to employees and that accrued tax liabilities were retroactive. Because of complexity and uncertainty, institutions contemplating establishing cafeteria benefits plans either for full- or part-time employees would be wise to engage an expert to assist in their construction.

Which Fringe Benefits Should Part-Timers Be Offered?

It is our contention that no single set of rules is applicable to a given institution's selection of a fringe benefits package for its part-time faculty. Instead, certain broad principles exist that should be balanced against the budget and the legal, philosophical, ethical, and traditional environment of an institution. The ideas developed in this section are designed to stimulate the thinking of persons at the institution rather than to lay down a strict framework that should be imposed.

Perhaps the broadest statement of principles in this area has been made by the AAUP.[6] The key recommendations made by its part-time committee in this area are as follow:

Colleges and universities should design policies on fringe benefits that reflect the varying commitments of part-time faculty.

Part-timers whose work is indistinguishable from comparable full-timers' with the exception of the proportion of time spent in an activity should have the opportunity to participate in nonmandatory fringe benefits on a prorated basis if their workload at their employing institution is continuous over several years.

Equal access should be given to all part-timers for fringe benefits such as medical and dental services, and, where possible, the employer's contribution should be prorated.

Institutions should endeavor to provide part-timers with access to retirement or life insurance coverage that has a vested component, as well as a number of other fringe benefits, for example, tuition remission.

In practice, many academic institutions have ignored these AAUP recommendations because of existing institutional policies, statutory limitations, board of trustee recalcitrance, administrative inertia, financial exigencies, etc. Yet, they serve an important role in laying out a common set of rules to guide the design of future programs.

The actual determination of whether part-time faculty will receive fringe benefits and what amount they will receive hinges on the institution's (and its governing agency's) philosophy concerning how part-timers can best be integrated into its professoriate and what constitutes equity for its employees. Each benefit described above has a cost, and some are quite significant. Hence, equity and professional considerations must be balanced against cost factors. Three criteria should guide institutional choice of specific benefits.

First, a chosen benefit should be cost-effective in the sense that its value-to-cost ratio should exceed that of a nonchosen one. This ratio should be determined by the administrator in charge of benefits selection in conjunction with the appropriate faculty benefits committee in a nonunionized school. In unionized institutions the choice will be the product of joint negotiations between the union and the administration. In some public institutions, the choice will be legislated from above and the ratio criterion may not apply.

Second, it is our contention a key factor that should determine a part-timer's fringe benefits levels is workload. Those who bear a large teaching load, the heavy-loaders, are more entitled to fringes than their less committed brethren. Third, access to other fringe benefits programs elsewhere should be a consideration in determining which benefits will be offered to part-timers.

With these criteria as a guide, we commend the following list of choices to institutions interested in exploring fringe benefits possibilities. The assumption is that if a particular benefit is not offered to full-time faculty, it is not a viable option for part-timers.

For *full-mooners (i.e., those with other jobs)*, institutions may want to consider the following benefits for part-time faculty:

1. Sick leave

2. Library privileges

3. Parking privileges

For *half-mooners (i.e., those employed part-time elsewhere) or hopeful full-timers,* institutions may want to examine awarding the following benefits to part-time faculty:

1. Pension plan (if the half-mooner or hopeful full-timer teaches at least one course per term with expectation of renewal)

2. Thrift plans

3. Health insurance (if the half-mooner or hopeful full-timer teaches at least one course per term with expectation of renewal)

4. Dental care (if the half-mooner or hopeful full-timer teaches at least one course per term with expectation of renewal)

5. Prescription drug plan (if the half-mooner or hopeful full-timer teaches at least one course per term with expectation of renewal)

6. Group life insurance plan (if the half-mooner or hopeful full-timer teaches at least one course per term with expectation of renewal)

7. Disability income plan (if the half-mooner or hopeful full-timer teaches at least one course per term with expectation of renewal)

8. Sick leave

9. Legal services plan (if the half-mooner or hopeful full-timer teaches at least one course per term with expectation of renewal)

10. Vision care (if the half-mooner or hopeful full-timer teaches at least one course per term with expectation of renewal)

11. Library privileges

12. Parking privileges

13. Sabbatical accrual (on a prorated basis)

14. Educational benefits (on a prorated basis)

15. Grants in support of scholarship (on a prorated basis)

For all other part-timers with no other access to fringe benefits, institutions may want to examine awarding the following benefits:

1. Pension plan (if the person teaches at least one course per term with some expectation of renewal)

2. Thrift plan

3. Health insurance (if the person teaches at least one course per term with some expectation of renewal)

4. Dental care (if the person teaches at least one course per term with some expectation of renewal)

5. Prescription drug plan (if the person teaches at least one course per term with some expectation of renewal)

6. Group insurance plan (if the person teaches at least one course per term with some expectation of renewal)

7. Disability income plan (if the person teaches at least one course with some expectation of renewal)

8. Library privileges

9. Parking privileges

10. Cafeteria benefits (if the institution offers these benefits to all staff and faculty, and the person teaches more than 1,000 hours per year, then these benefits could be explored for part-time faculty members)

Conclusions

While no national guidelines exist on the subject of whether fringe benefits should be awarded to part-time faculty, several general criteria make sense to apply. First, the choice should be made by individual institutions, taking into account such factors as their budget and their legal, philosophical, ethical, and traditional environment. Second, no fringes should be awarded to part-timers that are not available to full-timers. Third, fringes should be awarded on the basis of length of service to the institution and on workload. Fourth, access to fringe benefits at other places of work should be a consideration in determining whether to offer fringe benefits.

The choice of which benefits to provide should be based on the value-to-cost ratio of each fringe. In evaluating the choices, consideration should be given to factors like whether:

1. A fringe package is less costly than cash payments.

2. There are tax advantages in using fringe packages.

3. Group discounts can provide fringe benefits more cheaply than employees can receive them elsewhere.

4. Fringe benefits costs grow less rapidly than salary costs when inflation increases.

5. Fringe payments attract hard-to-get employees.

6. Fringe benefits increase productivity, loyalty, and/or institutional attachment.

7. Part-time coverage can be integrated into existing full-time plans.

8. Competitive institutions offer fringe packages.

Serious attention might be given to so-called *cafeteria* plans that enable faculty to assign their own values to each type of fringe. In almost all cases, part-time fringe benefits should be prorated to reflect workload.

In the final analysis, the question of how to handle the fringe benefits coverage of part-timers is part of the larger question of how part-time faculty should be integrated into their employing institution. The interests of an academic institution will be best served if this question is approached within the larger context of the question of how part-time faculty are to be treated by their employing institution.

Notes

1. Adapted from Howard P. Tuckman, and William D. Vogler, "The Fringes of a Fringe Group—Part-Timers in Academe," in *Part-Time Faculty Series,* Washington D.C.: AAUP, 1978, pp. 40–52.
2. 26 USCS 401(k).
3. 26 USCS 403(b).
4. 42 CFR 110.10.
5. U.S. Department of Labor, *Employee Benefits in Medium and Large Firms, 1982,* Bureau of Labor Statistics Bulletin 2176, August 1983.
6. "The Status of Part-Time Faculty," *Academe,* 67 (February–March 1981): 29–39.

—————— CHAPTER 7 ——————

Tenure and Part-Time Faculty Appointments

The idea that an institution might want to create tenure-track part-time positions for qualified part-time faculty may seem bizarre to some. This is particularly true in an era when declining enrollments and financial problems are forcing institutions to increase flexibility and reduce costs. Institutions may choose to grant tenure to part-timers for one or more of the following reasons:

1. To reward long-term service[1]

2. To retain desirable faculty who might otherwise be attracted to other institutions

3. To create a stronger attachment of part-time faculty to their institution.

4. To ensure academic freedom for all who teach

5. As a substitute for higher pay

75

6. In recognition that various courts have awarded tenure
to long-service part-time faculty.

Part-timers in turn are likely to prefer a tenure-track position for a number of reasons: to be assured of longer-term
employment, so that they know that time spent in course
preparation will be rewarded by a permanent position, and/or
as an indication of their value to their employer. Particularly
for those who have taught at an institution over a period of
years, tenure provides a tangible indication of status at the institution and of the fact that part-timers can have at least part of
the stature of their full-time counterparts. The granting of
tenure to part-timers is not restricted to lesser-known schools,
but has occurred at such high-quality institutions as Colgate,
Columbia, Cornell, Princeton, Wesleyan, Wisconsin, and Yale.

In this chapter we explore various issues associated with
formulating a policy toward the granting of tenure to part-
timers. Since no single policy is likely to cover all situations that
might arise at an institution, a major issue is how to determine
who will be eligible for tenure. The most common sources of eligibility are length of attachment to the institution, course load,
type of functions performed as a part-timer, and attachment to
the larger labor force. We consider each of these in the next
section. The categories selected are based on our discussion of
the Tobias and Tuckman taxonomies of part-timers presented
in Chapter 2.

Who Might Be Eligible for Tenure as a Part-Timer?

Perhaps the most likely reason for granting tenure to a part-
timer relates to attachment to the employing institution. Part-
timers who have spent several years at an institution usually are
aware of its tradition and culture, and their experience makes
them an asset to the institution. These part-timers often know
what is expected of them, have established a record as adequate
teachers, and have acquired a familiarity for the policies and
procedures of the institution. Particularly in medical schools, or
in nonurban 4-year colleges, such part-timers may be attached

to their employing institutions for many years. The awarding of tenure provides a way of showing gratitude to these people. However, a number of issues must be resolved if these persons are to receive tenure: (1) How many years and how many courses should a person teach to be eligible? (2) What does part-time tenure mean? (3) Under what circumstances can a part-timer be let go? A statement like the following might be used to describe institutional policy toward this group.

Part-Time Career Appointments for Regular Part-Time

Persons who have served 6 or more years as part-timers at this institution may be considered for tenure if they have taught [fill in appropriate number of classes, such as 24] and if they meet the standards for tenure laid out in the faculty handbook for full-time faculty.

A second class of part-timer that might be considered for tenure is one teaching more than one-half the course load of a full-time faculty member. Such persons might also be expected to perform duties beyond teaching, such as student advising, counseling, and even governance. The more the activities the part-timer performs, the closer his or her job becomes to that of a full-timer and the greater the rationale for providing a tenured position. An institution wishing to provide tenure for this type of part-timer might consider the following statement.

Part-Time Career Appointments for Persons with More Than Half-Time Loads

It is the policy of this institution to provide tenure track appointments for part-time faculty who have a load greater than one-half that of full-time faculty in their employing departments. Faculty eligible for such appointments will be considered using the standards for tenure laid out in the faculty handbook for full-time faculty.

A third type of part-timer who might be eligible for tenure is a full-time faculty member who wishes to assume a reduced load to spend time parenting. The following statement could be adopted to recognize this type of employment situation.

Part-Time Career Appointments for Parents:

To enable persons who are professionally committed to [university, college or 2-year college, as appropriate] service to care for their child(ren), part-time tenure track appointments may be made for eligible persons. Persons shall be eligible for this status only if they have one or more children under [an age can be selected that seems appropriate—the age of nine is one possibility] years of age at the beginning of the first academic year for which part-time career status is sought. These persons must be primarily responsible for the raising of the children and must plan to spend considerable time in this capacity. Eligible persons may be originally appointed to part-time career status, may change from full-time to part-time career status, or may change from part-time to full-time as their personal situation dictates and in consonance with the needs of the institution. Because of the purpose of this part-time career appointment, individuals are expected to care for their child(ren) and not engage in gainful employment outside the institution. Each year of part-time career status shall be counted as one-half year for full-time service in calculating the 7-year limit on appointments without tenure.

Finally, a fourth class of part-timer is the faculty member whose primary (or alternative) employment is elsewhere. This is the typical circumstance for a part-timer teaching at least half-time or more on a regular semester basis. Provisions for earning tenured status for such regular teaching could be established by adopting a policy statement similar to the following for institutional use.

1. Part-time service at less than one-half time shall not be counted in the probationary period of a tenure track part-time faculty member. Each year of service at the rate of at least one-half time but no more than three-quarters time shall count as one-half of a year for probationary purposes. Services at a rate greater than three-quarters time shall be counted as a full year. In no case

shall the probationary period exceed [a reasonable time frame is 12 years].

2. In all respects other than length of the probationary period, standards of teaching performance and scholarly qualities shall be the same as for full-time faculty.

3. If tenure is ultimately recommended by the teaching unit, the part-time faculty member will receive a prorata appointment with tenure, for example, one-half, three-quarters, two-thirds, etc. of a regular full-time faculty appointment.

The concept of providing tenure track part-time positions is one which should merit attention and interest from various academic institutions for at least 2 reasons.[2] First, it provides a means for integrating valued employees within the institutional framework in a way which supports the values and practices of the institution. Second, it offers a way of demonstrating that an institution provides an access channel to permanent teaching for its part-time employees. Third, it brings the part-timer out of the shadows and demonstrates that he or she is a faculty member with the rights and obligations this implies. Fourth, it makes it possible for institutions to demand many of the same qualities in their part-timers that they require in their full-timers.

Notes

1. Tuckman, Howard and Jaime Caldwell, "The Reward Structure for Part-Timers in Academe," *Journal of Higher Education*, 50 November-December, 1979. pp. 745–760.
2. Tuckman, Howard P., "Part-Time Faculty: Some Suggestions of Policy," *Change*, 13 January-February, 1981, pp. 8–10.

CHAPTER 8

The Professional Obligations of Part-Time Faculty

Job Description

Fundamental to the effective management of personnel is a clear understanding of the duties, tasks, and responsibilities of the jobs they hold within an organization. The process of analyzing and describing job content provides a wealth of information to both employers and employees. Job descriptions are critical to effective personnel management because

They make explicit the duties, tasks, and responsibilities of a job so that both the employer and employees are aware of what is expected on the job.

They aid in the determination of the relative worth of jobs and in the fairness of compensation.

They provide data to ensure that organizations are not violating the *equal pay for equal work* doctrine of the 1963 Equal Pay Act.

81

They aid in the recruitment of people capable of performing the specific duties, tasks, and responsibilities that the job requires.

They provide data that can be useful for career planning, advancement, and personal development.

They provide a baseline that the organization can use to document unsatisfactory employee performance.

They provide a standard against which acceptable performance can be judged.

Through careful analysis, a job or position description may be written for academic positions. A job description is defined as an enumeration of the work activities performed in a job, which usually includes information about other job-related aspects such as working conditions, task priorities, and accountability.

The following, a generic description of the part-timer's activities, was derived by analysis of the functions a part-timer performs. It can be adapted to fit the requirements of most academic institutions.

Job Description for a Typical Part-Time Faculty Member

I. Philosophy

The relationship of a part-time faculty member to his or her students is one of teacher to student. The part-time faculty member should adhere to the following fundamental principles that are pertinent to his or her teaching position:

1. Objective, unbiased, nonopinionated research and teaching form the basis for academic freedom.

2. Behavioral learning objectives are the foundation for designing and teaching a course.

II. Part-Time Faculty Functions

A. Relating to Teaching:

The goal of a part-time faculty member is to educate the total person.

1. Course Planning
   The part-time faculty member will
   a. Use behavioral learning objectives in designing course content
   b. Use appropriate instructional media for all courses taught
   c. Prepare thoroughly for all courses taught
   d. Adapt various teaching techniques to meet class and individual learning needs
   e. Assist the teaching unit in preparing pertinent and clear syllabi for his or her course(s)
2. Course Implementation
   The part-time faculty member will
   a. Meet scheduled classes or make institutionally acceptable alternative arrangements
   b. Foster a climate of inquiry through free expression and class interaction
   c. Facilitate interdisciplinary experiences for students
   d. Meet scheduled office hours for student consultations
3. Course Evaluation
   The part-time faculty member will
   a. Use evaluative devices to measure teaching effectiveness (e.g., questionnaires, tests, etc.)
   b. Use evaluative devices for course effectiveness
   c. Report student progress and grades as required within the time frame specified

B. Relating to the Institution
   1. Organizational responsibilities at all levels
      The part-time faculty member will
      a. Strive for open communication in the classroom
      b. Provide constructive feedback to students and administrative personnel
      c. Be prepared to act as a teaching unit resource in shaping departmental goals, developing curricula, and ensuring course coordination

C. Relating to the Community

The part-time faculty member will be supportive of the activities of the institution by maintaining

1. Positive relationships with other educational institutions
2. Positive relationships with community groups
3. Outside relationships with professionals and employers interested in employing or otherwise placing students in internships or other permanent positions

D. Relating to Professional Groups

The part-time faculty member will participate as assigned in orientations, professional development programs, and graduation ceremonies.

E. Relating to Institutional Accountability

The part-time faculty member will

1. Be responsible to the appropriate supervisor(s) within the institution
2. Maintain appropriate course materials for evaluation by supervisors

Teaching Responsibilities

From this generic job description, specific responsibilities can be assigned to part-time faculty. The following statement outlines the responsibilities that a part-timer has in teaching. It is meant as a departure point for further consideration by those responsible for formulating such a statement.

Sample Statement of Part-Time Faculty Teaching Responsibilities

The responsibilities of part-time faculty are as follow

1. The assigned classes in the area of employment should be conducted in accordance with the catalogue description and the policies set forth by the institution.

2. Behavioral learning objectives should be developed for each course. A behavioral learning objective specifies the changes

in student behavior expected as a result of that person taking the course. A model for writing behavioral learning objectives is as follows:

> By the end of this course, the student should be able to [demonstrate some *performance*] [measured by some *criterion*] [under some *condition*]. An example is: By the end of this course, the student should be able to write a complex BASIC computer program that is operational without referring to a reference text.

3. Every class, including the final examination, should be held the full scheduled number of minutes in the assigned classroom. Every scheduled class should be met and taught even if this is inconvenient, and classes should be canceled only as a last resort. Whenever a part-time faculty member is to be absent from, or late for, a class, or whenever he or she must leave the institution before meeting all classes assigned, proper notification should be made to the immediate academic supervisor. Missed classes must be made up. There are various levels of "coverage" in order of preference:

> The class meets and is taught, or the examination is given, so that the syllabus is carried forward in spite of the absence. This should be especially possible in multi-section courses where different instructors and sections can be assumed to be fairly close together in a common syllabus.

> The class meets and is continued throughout the period by discussion, review, in-class written assignment, or similar instructional technique.

> The class meets, roll is taken, and the class is then dismissed for further research or other written work previously assigned.

> The class is canceled.

Each part-time faculty member is authorized one [paid or unpaid, depending upon institutional preference—it is suggested this be *paid*] absence per semester, on a noncumulative basis, as the result of illness. Such an absence is defined as one that occurs on any 1 calendar day, during either a regular semester or a summer term, on which the part-time faculty member is scheduled to teach. For absences not attributable to illness or involving more than 1 calendar day per semester and attributable to illness, the responsibility for financial arrangements for a guest instructor rests with the part-time faculty member.

4. Standards of teaching that are worthy of accreditation must be maintained.

5. Means of improving instruction should be sought out through professional meetings, societies, workshops, and the current literature of the field. Aid and assistance in these matters may be obtained from colleagues, department chairpersons, program coordinators, academic supervisors, and learning resource personnel.

6. Insofar as possible, teaching methods should be adjusted to student needs.

7. Mid-term and final grade reports must be submitted *on time*.

8. Copies of the final examination and the syllabus, reading lists, and other instructional materials of like nature should be submitted to the appropriate academic supervisor.

9. Faculty must be available for student consultation for each course taught in accordance with institutional guidelines.

Issues

The materials presented suggest that an academic institution should be able to provide a well-defined description of the job content of a part-time teaching position without undue difficulty. It is our belief that the time spent in preparing such a description will be amply rewarded in terms of

More rapid orientation of part-time faculty to the institutional environment

Less chance for misunderstandings, which give rise to lower-quality or the wrong type of teaching

Less chance of lawsuits based on allegations of unclear definition of responsibilities.

Better employee relations through an explicit recognition of part-timers' need for orientation to the policies of their employer

There are, however, several issues that should be addressed by anyone undertaking to write a handbook before a decision is made to adopt a model such as the one proposed. These include the following:

Whether an institution has such a diverse set of uses for its part-timers that extensive "special circumstances" govern its expectations (e.g., as in a case with part-timers at medical, law, nursing, and engineering schools). If so, the description will have to take each of these into account.

Whether nonteaching duties are envisioned of part-timers. In some institutions, part-timers spend time in supervisory and other administrative functions. Recognition of these functions should be made in the professional obligations section of the handbook.

Whether any administrative regulations restrict the ability of the institution to formulate rules (e.g., if board of regents rules affect the policies of an institution).

Whether the policies should be worked out unilaterally by the employer or whether part-time employees should be given an input.

Whether the expectations for part-timers should be the same as those of full-timers (e.g., should they be as well-prepared in class?).

Careful attention to the details of what constitutes the professional obligations of a part-timer can pay off later in terms of a more harmonious relationship between the part-timers at an institution and their employer.[1] The goal in formulating this, as well as all other, sections of the part-time handbook should be to meld the professional needs and interests of part-timers with the needs and interests of their employing institutions.

Notes

1. For another view on the relationship of part-time faculty and their employing institutions, see Richard H. Potter, "Part-Time Faculty: Employees or Contractors?" *Journal of the College and University Personnel Association,* 35 (Fall 1984):22–27.

CHAPTER 9

Evaluation and Promotion Criteria for Part-Time Faculty

Over 40 years ago, Logan Wilson, then-President of the University of Texas, wrote in his book, *The Academic Man:*

> Indeed, it is no exaggeration to say that the most critical problem confronted in the social organization of any [institution of higher education] is the proper evaluation of faculty services, and giving due recognition through the impartial assignment of status.[1]

The perspective that Wilson took so many years ago is still valid today. The goal of an academic institution should be to establish promotion and evaluation guidelines for its part-timers that meet the following broad objectives. They should be

Well articulated and easily accessible

Equitable and reflective of prevailing campus norms and traditions regarding evaluation and promotion

Consistent with the hiring criteria used to select part-timers and the workload and expectations placed upon them

Designed to ensure that part-time faculty receive the recognition and status deemed appropriate for them

In practice, realization of these goals requires careful planning, forethought, and a willingness to design a set of evaluation and promotion policies integrated with other policies regarding the treatment of part-timers. We shall deal with several ways to accomplish this integration in this chapter.

Establishing Policies to Evaluate Part-Time Faculty Members

A part-timer's introduction to his or her employing institution's policies should begin at the time he or she is hired. Information should be provided on the institution's evaluation procedures, how often they are applied, and the person(s) who will apply them. The newly hired part-timer needs to understand how the results of regularly conducted evaluations are to be used and whether favorable evaluation will lead to academic promotion, higher compensation, and/or other rewards.

Evaluations of part-time faculty should include at least six components.[2]

STUDENT ASSESSMENTS

Student assessments of teaching should be an input into the overall evaluation process. In institutions that have a student evaluation procedure for rating full-time faculty personnel actions, evaluations should also be conducted of part-time faculty performance and effectiveness. In institutions without such evaluations, serious attention should be given to adding student evaluations to the part-time evaluation process as a low-cost way of obtaining feedback on performance.

WRITTEN APPRAISALS OF PART-TIMER PERFORMANCE

Written appraisals should be regularly conducted by the head of the relevant teaching unit. An appraisal should normally take into account

Class size

Number of preparations for classes (applicable only to part-time faculty who teach multiple sections during a semester or quarter)

Innovative use of experimental teaching methods, if any

The difficulty of the subject matter (while this type of determination is necessarily subjective, it is nonetheless appropriate to include)

Whether the part-timer's classes are mandatory or optional

Counseling and advisement activities if advisement is part of a part-time faculty member's duties and contractual requirements

Development of new curricula

Observation of teaching effectiveness through classroom visitation by either a part-timer's peers or by a suitable administrator (e.g., department chairperson)

PUBLICATION OF MATERIALS IN A RESPECTABLE ACADEMIC OR TRADE JOURNAL

If publication took place during the contract period, and if it was in the field in which the part-timer teaches, this should be noted in the part-timer's employment file. Normally, a part-timer is not hired, or expected, to publish as a condition of employment. However, such publication not only brings credit to the institution, but also provides evidence of scholarly productivity and conversance with a field of knowledge. Hence, it is an element that should be taken into consideration at evaluation time. Moreover, if a part-timer is a hopeful full-timer, as discussed in Chapter 2, then evidence of publication may be an important factor in both promotion and consideration for full-time faculty status.

SERVICE RENDERED TO THE INSTITUTION OR COMMUNITY

A part-timer is normally not expected to devote additional time to his or her employing institution beyond the specific teaching or research obligations written into the employment contract. Where additional service is offered to the institution or community, this should be noted in the part-timer's employment record.

LENGTH OF SERVICE

For part-time faculty members who have spent many years teaching a specialized course or for those who have spent time at an entry-level grade and who are used on a regular basis to teach courses, length of service is a reasonable criterion for promotion. The inclusion of such a criterion if the institution applies this to full-timers serves both to ensure equitable treatment of part-timers and to confer a measure of legitimacy on the services part-timers offer. It implicitly assumes that when a part-timer is regularly used for teaching, his or her performance has been judged to be satisfactory. Thus, if this policy is adopted, it should be used in conjunction with yearly evaluation of part-time faculty.

INSTITUTIONAL GOVERNANCE ACTIVITIES

Institutional governance activities can take many forms, and each should be evaluated on its own merits. Normally, part-timers are not expected to serve on faculty committees, have office hours, advise students, or attend faculty meetings. Those who perform these activities should receive recognition for their extra effort. Which activities are recognized should be a matter for each institution to resolve, based on its policies toward full-timers and its perception of which are the valuable activities for part-timers to perform. For example, at least one author has recommended that part-time faculty be required to attend departmental meetings on a regular basis.[3] If an institution follows this recommendation, then an issue arises as to whether to recognize attendance at departmental meetings in the evaluation process. How an institution deals with this question will affect how motivated its part-timers will be to undertake these additional activities.

Options for Evaluating and Promoting Part-Time Faculty

Academic administrators need guidelines for establishing a useful set of criteria for evaluating and ultimately promoting part-time faculty. We recognize this area as probably one of the most diffuse of those covered in this book. Institutional policies are affected by a myriad of factors such as availability of qualified part-timers, availability of institutional funds, union status–bargaining unit composition, public or private ownership, institutional image, specialization and types of courses, and the like. Notwithstanding these sources of diversity, an institution needs to grapple with the thorny issues of evaluation and promotion to provide its part-time faculty with a sense of equity and a feeling that their efforts are recognized. We have developed a general model helpful in exploring the criteria to be imposed in evaluating and promoting faculty. Chapter 2 discussed two part-time faculty taxonomies presented in the Tuckman and Tobias papers. For the purpose of discussing the evaluation and promotion of part-time faculty, we use the Tuckman taxonomy presented below. The reader who wishes a refresher on this taxonomy should refer to Chapter 2.

Part-timers can be semi-retired, students, hopeful full-timers, full-mooners, part-mooners, or homeworkers. For persons who fall into the hopeful full-timer, students, and semi-retired categories, it appears appropriate that part-timer evaluations should include the items discussed earlier in this chapter. We have placed the items into a hierarchy of importance that makes sense to us. However, each institution will have to assess whether or not this hierarchy ("pecking order") is useful based on its own institutional culture and needs.

Evaluation Items for Hopeful Full-Timers, Students, and Semi-Retired in Descending Order of Importance

1. Written appraisals of a part-timer's performance, which should include at the minimum
   - Class size
   - Whether the class is mandatory or optional
   - Number of preparations for classes
   - Classroom visitations
   - Difficulty of the subject matter
   - Counseling and advisement activities
   - Development of new curricula
   - Innovative use of experimental teaching methods
2. Student evaluations of part-timer's teaching effectiveness
3. Institutional governance activities
4. Services rendered the institution
5. Publication record

Persons falling into the remaining three categories of the Tuckman taxonomy (full-mooners, part-mooners, and homeworkers) could be appraised on the basis of student evaluations and longevity. Once again, we list each item in the sequence of importance that seems to make the most sense. Obviously, other evaluative elements can be added to the following model, and some readers may object to our lumping together those with full- and part-time employment with homeworkers.

Evaluation Items for Full-Mooners, Part-Mooners, and Homeworkers in Descending Order of Importance

1. Student evaluations of teaching

2. Length of service

3. Classroom visitation

Teaching Evaluations

Several studies suggest that institutions that evaluate full-timers for teaching effectiveness are likely to do the same for part-timers. Table 9.1 reveals that such evaluation is fairly wide-spread at public community 2-year colleges.[4]

Despite the prevalence of evaluations of part-timers, one set

TABLE 9.1
Frequency of Evaluation of Part-Time Faculty by Type

TYPE OF EVALUATION	USE OF EVALUATION				
	Always	Often	Occasionally	Seldom	Never
Student	54.0	27.0	11.9	0	7.1
Self	15.3	18.6	21.2	24.6	20.3
Peer	10.0	18.3	16.7	25.0	30.0
Administrator	47.5	30.3	10.7	4.1	7.4

Note: All figures are expressed in percentages and the total number of colleges in the sample is 121.

of authors made the following comments in a recent book concerning part-time faculty in U.S. higher education:

> The prevailing questions about the quality of instruction
> provided by part-timers remain as unanswered and unans-
> werable as the same questions are when asked about full-time
> faculty. Results, where they are available, suggest two gener-
> alizations: On global measures of quality, student ratings
> produce no differences between part- and full-time instruc-
> tors. However, from detailed descriptions of instructional be-
> havior, it appears clear that part-timers do different sorts of
> things in the classroom. Interpretation depends on the posi-
> tion and perspective of the assessor. Students, especially ma-
> ture adults, appreciate and value the pragmatism and realism
> part-timers often bring to the classroom. But full-timers see
> the same behavior and decry the erosion of standards
> represented by less required writing and library research for
> part-timers. In other words, there are practical, technical,
> and conceptual problems in trying to evaluate part-timers'
> teaching performance and to compare it with some useful
> and meaningful standard. In general, it is a set of problems
> most institutions ignore.[5]

One institution that chose not to ignore these problems was
Regis College in Denver, Colorado. A model of the indicators
of an effective institutional evaluation system follows, based on
one used at Regis.[6]

Indicators of an Effective Part-Time Faculty Evaluation System

1. A workable evaluation system should measure work, not
   the worker. It should concentrate on the performance of
   agreed-upon goals and focus on success in planning,
   organizing, implementing, and evaluating.

2. It is a living system that is contemporary and operational.

3. It is as objective as possible with pre-set, pre-agreed-

upon standards that are qualitatively and quantitatively verifiable.

4. It is acceptable to the personnel involved.

5. It is constructive in tone and leads to growth and development. Coaching and development are basic to the system.

6. It provides a basis for modifying or changing behavior as necessary to improve performance.

7. It motivates professional employees by providing feedback on how they are doing.

8. It provides a research and reference base for personnel decisions.

The Regis College evaluation employs specific criteria to evaluate its full-time and part-time faculty:[7]
1. Teaching experience
2. Teaching effectiveness. Attributes and characteristics used to assess effectiveness are
   a. Command of one's subject
   b. Ability to organize subject matter and to present it clearly, logically, and imaginatively
   c. Knowledge of current developments in one's discipline
   d. Ability to relate one's subject to other areas of knowledge
   e. Ability to provoke and broaden student interest in the subject matter
   f. Ability to utilize effective teaching methods and strategies
   g. Possession of the attributes of integrity, industry, open-mindedness, and objectivity in teaching
Regis College uses the following sources to assess teaching effectiveness: self-ratings, supervisor ratings, peer ratings, review of course syllabi by peers inside or outside the college, and student ratings.
3. Service to the college

4. Research and creative work
5. Professional activities
6. Service to the community
7. Teaching improvement activities
8. Service to the student body

Performance evaluation is important to ensure that high-quality standards are maintained in the classroom. Institutions would be well served to adopt an evaluation system that guarantees its students are receiving a learning experience of high quality. The following abbreviated policy statements are suggested as ones that could be adapted to an institution's existing teaching evaluation policies and procedures.

Sample Statement for Evaluation of Part-Time Faculty

1. Part-time faculty shall be evaluated at least once during the academic year. New part-time faculty shall be evaluated within 6 weeks of their initial contract.
2. Part-time faculty shall be evaluated by appropriate student groups and by the teaching unit supervisor.
3. Times and dates for evaluation procedures will be promulgated in advance.
4. The teaching unit supervisor shall review the evaluation with the part-time faculty member. The results of the evaluation will be filed in the part-time faculty member's personnel folder.
5. Part-time faculty will be evaluated using the same evaluation instruments as are used for full-time faculty.

Promotion Criteria

Once part-timers have been evaluated, they can be considered for what Wilson called "the impartial assignment of status." Persons meeting the criteria established for promotion from entry to middle and from middle to senior levels could be considered based on either performance or seniority. (See Chapter 4 for a discussion on making part-time faculty appointments.) Seniority makes sense for the long-term employee. Promotion provides a way for his or her institution to offer status as a reward for longevity. Conversely, part-time faculty who have a lesser length of service at an institution may be considered for promotion on the basis of their meritorious performance. This provides a status-based incentive for outstanding service or productivity.

Conclusions

It is of considerable importance for an institution to develop a written and well-articulated set of policies regarding the evaluation of part-timers for retention, promotion, and compensation purposes. The specific standards used in such evaluation will vary depending on the philosophy of the institution, its constraints, and its environment. Nonetheless, several basic criteria should be used in evaluation, including student assessments, written appraisals of part-timer performance, publication of materials in respectable journals, service rendered to the institution or community, length of service, and institutional governance activities. The same criteria should be applied to all classes of part-timers if the institution wishes to use a taxonomy based upon either part-timer needs (the Tuckman taxonomy) or institutional needs (the Tobias taxonomy). Clearly, the weights assigned to each of the chosen criteria will differ depending on the taxonomy, but considerable flexibility exists in designing evaluation criteria for part-timers, and individual institutions are likely to develop their own models.

It is our belief that considerable gains are to be had from beginning with the broad criteria presented above. In particular, the policies used for evaluation should be well articulated, easily accessible, equitable, reflective of prevailing campus norms regarding evaluation and promotion, consistent with the hiring criteria used to select part-timers and the workload and expectations placed upon them, and designed to ensure that part-time faculty receive the recognition and status deemed appropriate for them. By specifically addressing these criteria, an institution can ensure that its part-time policies will enhance faculty productivity and reduce the uncertainties that the occupants of part-time positions face.

Notes

1. Logan Wilson, *The Academic Man: A Study in the Sociology of a Profession,* New York: Oxford University Press, 1942, p. 112.
2. For an interesting discussion on criteria for evaluating part-time faculty members, see Mary M. Norman, "Advice and Recommendations: Improving the Work Environment for Part-Timers," *AAHE Bulletin,* 37 (October 1984):13–14.
3. *Ibid.,* p. 14.
4. Alan John Schreibmeier. "An Investigation of Part-Time Faculty Staff Development in Public Community Junior Colleges in the United States," Ph.D. dissertation, University of Texas at Austin, 1980.
5. David W. Leslie, Samuel E. Killiams, and G. Manny Gunne, *Part-Time Faculty in American Higher Education,* New York: Praeger 1982.
6. The elements in this system were gleaned from faculty evaluation workshop materials provided to the authors by Dr. Thomas A. Emmet of Regis College, Denver, Colarado.
7. *Ibid.*

CHAPTER 10

Part-Time Faculty and Due Process

Due Process Defined

The primary purpose of the due process clauses of the Fifth and the Fourteenth Amendments to the U.S. Constitution, as they have been interpreted by various courts, is to ensure that individuals are not deprived of certain basic rights—life, liberty, and property—in an unfair or arbitrary manner. The rights and privileges protected by these amendments are as follow:

The right to be heard with respect to economic and professional interests in a meaningful and effective way.

The right to petition for redress of economic and professional grievances in a meaningful and effective way.

The right to bargain individually or collectively with one's employer with respect to the terms and conditions of employment.

The right to associate together through a chosen representative for the purpose of negotiating with an institution with respect to economic and professional interests on an equal basis.

The right to confront one's accuser, to have an impartial and fair hearing, and to have the right of an appeal to an impartial adjudicator.

If an employee believes that he or she has not been accorded due process in terms of any of these rights, he or she has the right to voice a grievance (complaint) to an appropriate authority. If the employee is covered by a union contract, the grievance may charge the contract has been violated and it may seek some form of redress for ills caused by the violation. If not, the grievance may allege violation of institutional policies or practices. At a minimum, a grievance will charge that some type of injustice has been perpetrated by the employer and seeks either compensation, elimination of an unfair practice or rule, prohibition of a future action, or some combination of the these.

Academic institutions provide various avenues for aggrieved employees to voice their complaints. Some provide for a faculty committee to hear the complaint and make recommendations, others have a person or persons who hear the alleged violations and make recommendations, and still others employ a process that uses both faculty and administrators to hear complaints. All institutions share the goal of providing academic employees with a means to be heard and a way of receiving redress when this is appropriate. In virtually all cases, a grievance system calls for a good-faith relationship between employer and employee. A commitment of both parties to make fair compromises based upon mutually satisfactory and reasonable interpretations of employment policies is indispensable to a successful grievance system. A typical grievance procedure for full-time faculty might establish such steps as the following:

A full-time faculty member with a grievance against his or

her institution first takes it to the department chairperson. [Note: This act places the grieved issue into the hands of a person representing *both* the institution and the faculty. A department chairperson is charged with carrying out and enforcing institutional policies, but he or she is (or should be) an advocate for the aggrieved faculty member when a difference exists between academic policy and actual practice. The conflict in the department chairperson's role can affect the due process accorded at this stage.]

If the grievance cannot adequately be resolved at the departmental level, it may then go to the appropriate dean who will consider it and make a ruling. If this is disputed, depending on the organization, the grievance will then go to the vice-presidential and/or presidential levels. After its consideration there, if it remains unsettled, the president may refer it to an executive committee of the faculty senate, which in turn may assign it to a standing committee on faculty welfare or to a subcommittee on faculty grievances. The final step at the institution is for the president to decide whether the administation's or the senate's earlier disposition of it was correct. If the grievant is still unhappy with the outcome, a court case is his or her final recourse.

This lengthy and uncertain process is hardly conducive to speedy deliberations, and it can be a frustrating experience unless a detailed timetable is announced and adhered to. The legalistic overtones of full-time faculty grievance processes often stymie quick resolution of the issues, and legalisms can affect both unionized and nonunionized institutions.[1] The judicious handling of legitimate complaints, either inside or outside formal grievance steps, is a sound foundation for sustaining good human relationships, but this may not always be obtained in the preceding process.[2] For this reason, the full-time model may not be an ideal one for providing avenues of redress for part-timers. Yet, equitable personnel management practices suggest that a part-time faculty member with a grievance should be accorded opportunities similar to those granted his or her full-time counterparts.[3] The following procedures recognize these problems by suggesting a process that provides specific time periods for the resolution of grievances at each level. We believe that the use of such a timetable improves the process by rendering it more timely.

Rights Accorded Part-Time Faculty under Due Process

Equitable part-time faculty grievance procedures should at the minimum embody the following philosophies:

> The basic objective of a grievance procedure is to achieve sound and fair settlements. It should not be to pit one side against the other with the attitude of winner take all, nor should the process be construed as zero sum.
>
> Grievances should be considered as an aid in the process of discovering and removing causes of institutional discontent.
>
> The willingness of an institution to devote the necessary time and attention to handling the disposition of grievances is crucial to the effective functioning of the process.

The Steps in Handling a Part-Time Faculty Member's Grievance

Under a typical collective bargaining agreement between *unionized* faculty and their institution, grievance handling takes the following general format:

1. A limited time span is provided for submitting a grievance.
2. A relatively short formal procedure exists for resolving the grievance. A typical four-step procedure would be:
   a. A conference between the part-time faculty member, the department chairperson, and the union representative.
   b. A conference between the dean and middle union management.

    c. A conference between institutional top management (the president or his/her designee) and top union leadership.

    d. A final resolution by the Board of Trustees or Regents having input from the top union leadership. Approximately 90 percent of all academic grievance procedures stop at this point.

3. If these conferences fail to resolve the grievance, in the 10 percent of grievance procedures that provide for outside arbitration, then an impartial and skilled arbitrator is appointed to hear the case and to make a reasoned decision based on the provisions of the written agreement between the institution and the bargaining unit.

4. The arbitrator's award is final and binding upon both the union and the institution.

Faculty Grievance Policy Considerations

It is difficult to formulate a single part-time faculty grievance policy statement that satisfies the widely varying needs of

1. Public institutions where grievance filing procedures are prescribed

2. Unionized institutions with strict contractual relationships with faculty members

3. Nonunionized institutions having their own cultures and self-developed procedures

The following comprehensive statement accommodates these varying needs in as best a manner as we were able to devise. It outlines provisions for establishing a grievance procedure ending in arbitration that encompasses virtually all contingencies and all types of part-time faculty. We expect that institutions wishing to adopt a part-time faculty grievance procedure will modify our wording to reflect their needs and requirements.

Sample Grievance and Arbitration Procedures for Part-Time Faculty Members

This institution encourages prompt and informal resolution of part-time faculty complaints. It also wishes to provide orderly procedures for their satisfactory adjustment.

A. Definition of a grievance by a part-time faculty member

    1. A *grievance* shall mean a complaint by a part-time faculty member that he or she has been treated unfairly or inequitably by reason of any act or condition that is contrary to established policy or practice.

    2. An individual part-time faculty member may handle his or her own grievance case, or in a unionized institution may be represented by the union.

    3. Neither the grievant nor the institution shall be represented by counsel in the first steps of the grievance procedure. Part-time faculty members may be assisted and have present a union representative if unionized. Either party may be represented by counsel only at the fifth step of the grievance procedure.

B. General Procedures

    1. Step 1

        a. A part-time faculty member may present a grievance concerning himself or herself (with assistance from the union representative if unionized) no later than 10 working days following his or her knowledge of or notification of the act, event, or commencement of the condition that is the basis for the grievance.

        b. The grievance shall be presented in the first instance to the departmental chairperson. If an *informal* presentation of the grievance to the chairperson does not result in an adjustment or settlement of the grievance, the grievant and the department chairperson shall designate in writing on a *grievance fact sheet* the facts relating to the issue or issues raised by the grievance. The grievance fact sheet will include the facts agreed to *and* the facts not agreed to by both parties but that should be taken into consideration by the departmental chairperson in evaluating the grievance and rendering a decision.

    c. All *formal* grievances to the departmental chairperson shall be in writing and shall be signed by the grievant (and the union president or appropriate designee, if unionized). The union may indicate on the grievance fact sheet whether it supports or does not support the grievance.

    d. The department chairperson shall evaluate informal and formal grievances and render a decision *in writing* within 3 working days after its receipt.

2. Step 2

    a. If the grievance is still not settled to the satisfaction of the grievant, it may be submitted to the dean of the teaching unit within 5 working days of the decision by the departmental chairperson.

    b. A written grievance presented to the dean shall also include a statement as to why the disposition of the grievance proposed by the departmental chairperson is unsatisfactory.

    c. If the grievant and the union president or his or her designee (if unionized) request, the dean shall accord them an opportunity to state their views on the grievance.

    d. The dean shall communicate his or her written decision to all parties concerned as promptly as possible, but not later than 5 working days after receiving the grievance.

3. Step 3

    a. Within 5 working days after receipt of the written decision by the dean, if the grievance is still not settled to the satisfaction of the grievant, it may be submitted by the grievant to the appropriate administrative authority established by the institution. This authority will appoint a grievance adjustment board.

    b. Proceedings before the grievance adjustment board shall be informal, and formal rules of evidence shall not apply. Any testimony and documentary evidence relevant to a determination shall be admitted as evidence by the board and considered by the board in its deliberations.

    c. Copies of documents to be presented to the grievance adjustment board and the names of witnesses to be called by the parties shall be exhanged by the parties not less than 5 working days prior to the scheduled commencement of the proceeding.

d. Proceedings before the grievance adjustment board shall be closed except to the parties directly involved.

e. The grievance adjustment board shall schedule proceedings on the grievance not later than 10 working days after the decision of the dean is appealed and shall render its decision no later than 10 working days following the close of the proceedings. The board may, at its discretion, hold the record of the submission of written arguments open for a reasonable period following the close of oral testimony. The decision of the board shall be in writing and shall contain specific findings of fact and conclusions. The decision of a majority of the board shall be controlling. The board decision shall be distributed to all parties within 25 working days from the time of initial receipt of the grievance by the Board.

4. Step 4

    a. If the grievance is still not settled to the satisfaction of the grievant, it may be submitted by the grievant to the provost of the institution within 10 working days after the decision of the grievance adjustment board is issued.

    b. The appeal to the provost shall be signed and in writing. It shall specifically state the act or condition and the grounds on which the grievance is based. It will include a statement of why the disposition of the grievance at Steps 1–3 was unsatisfactory.

    c. The provost or his or her designee if so requested, shall promptly meet with the grievant (and the union president or designee, if unionized) on the appeal.

    d. The provost or his or her designee shall communicate the decision in writing to all parties to the grievance. This decision shall be rendered not later than 10 working days after the written appeal has been received by the provost.

5. Step 5

    a. The grievant may appeal the provost's decision to an outside arbitrator for arbitration in accordance with the American Arbitration Association rules within 40 working days after the provost has rendered a decision. The outside arbitrator shall be selected by mutual agreement by the grievant (grievant's union, if unionized) and the institution.

b. The proceeding will be initiated by filing with the provost and the selected arbitrator a notice of arbitration. The arbitrator shall hold a hearing within 20 working days of receiving notice of arbitration. Five working days' notice shall be given to all parties of the time and place of the hearing.

c. Arbitration shall be conducted without a court reporter, unless either party desires one and intends to make use of a transcript for the purpose of presenting the case before the arbitrator. Such party shall pay the costs of the reporter and shall furnish at its cost copies of transcripts to the other party and to the arbitrator. Arbitration shall be conducted without posthearing briefs. If oral argument is necessary, it shall be made within 20 working days of completion of taking testimony.

d. The arbitrator shall issue his or her decision not later than 20 working days from the date of completion of the taking of testimony or of submission of the written record or of closing oral argument, whichever is latest. The arbitrator's decision shall be in writing and shall contain specific findings of fact and conclusions.

e. The arbitrator's fees and expenses shall be shared equally by all parties.

f. The decision of the arbitrator will be accepted in good faith by both parties to the grievance, and both parties will abide by it.

g. The arbitrator shall limit his or her decision strictly to the application and interpretation of the institution's written policies, practices, and any agreement, if unionized. The arbitrator will be without power or authority to make any decisions

    (i) contrary to, inconsistent with, or modifying or varying in any way institutional policies, practices, or agreements, if unionized; or

    (ii) limiting or interfering in any way with the

powers, duties, and responsibilities of the institution under applicable law.

h. Neither the institution nor the grievant (union, if unionized) will appeal an arbitration award to the courts unless the arbitrator is believed by either party to have acted illegally.

C. Time Limits

   1. Failure at any step of the procedure to communicate the decision on a grievance within the specified time limits shall permit the grievant to proceed to the next step. Failure at any step of the procedure to appeal a grievance to the next step within the specified time limits shall be deemed acceptance of the decision rendered at that step.

   2. The time limits specified in the grievance may be extended in any specific instance by mutual agreement in writing.

   3. Service under this grievance procedure may be made by personal service, duly receipted, or by certified mail, return receipt requested. If the grievant is represented by a union, service upon the union at its post office address shall constitute service upon the grievant.

Termination

An educational institution has the legal right to discharge a part-time faculty member for genuine economic reasons and/or unsatisfactory work performance. However, and as a cautionary note, institutions should maintain adequate records that support all allegations of unsatisfactory work. Such records would be used, particularly in a unionized situation, in establishing that a discharge was for cause and not for antiunion purposes. Without adequate documentation, and where a unionized part-time faculty member's explanation of work performance is plausible, a discharge would probably be construed as a violation of federal and/or state labor laws.

Institutions should take special care to ensure that their part-time faculty contracts, part-time faculty handbooks and other documentation make no statements that would provide expectations for reappointment or permanency of employment. Where an institution has adequately documented its rationale and reasons for terminating a part-time faculty member, statements that could weaken the right to terminate "at will" could expose the institution to challenge or even litigation.

When termination is judged necessary, the part-time faculty member should be told on a face-to-face basis the reason for termination. Simultaneously, a letter formally notifying the part-time faculty member of the termination with supporting statements should be provided. The letter, signed by an officer of the institution, should clearly spell out the reasons for termination. If the reasons are economic in nature, this should be stated along with a phrase stating that the institution's decision to terminate the services of the part-time faculty member was without prejudice. If, however, the termination is because of unsatisfactory classroom performance, student complaints, poor teaching, or inadequate classroom preparation, the institution owes the part-time faculty member a specific explanation as to the reasoning behind such an adverse personnel action.

Conclusions

The preceding agreement demonstrates that it is possible to formulate a grievance procedure that reduces the lengthy delays characterizing many existing grievance procedures. The adoption of a model leading to arbitration such as the one proposed here for part-timers would require some institutions to modify their overall procedures. This would not necessarily be bad if it resulted in a decrease in the number of layers of decision making and consequently in the time required to process a grievance through the system. The adoption of any grievance procedure for part-timers is costly in terms of both faculty and staff time and resources; so an institution must decide whether it wants to establish a separate system for part-timers, subject them to its existing procedures, or exclude them entirely. It is our view that the short-term savings obtained by totally excluding part-timers from any grievance procedure may turn out to be more costly in the long run than the adoption of a procedure such as the one described above, particularly if the absence of an adequate procedure gives rise to lengthy courtroom litigation. The time to provide for adequate due processs is before the charge is made that there is none.

Notes

1. Joseph W. Garbarino, *Faculty Bargaining*, New York: McGraw-Hill, 1975. p. 152.
2. George W. Angell, Edward P. Kelly, Jr., and associates, *Handbook of Faculty Bargaining*, San Francisco: Jossey-Bass, 1977, p. 382.
3. For an excellent discussion on this topic, see David W. Leslie, "Part-Time Faculty: Legal and Collective Bargaining Issues," *AAHE Bulletin*, 37 (October 1984): 8–12.

CHAPTER 11

The Part-Time Faculty Collective Bargaining Unit

The decision to establish a unit for the purposes of bargaining collectively is rarely made by an academic institution. More often than not, the employees of an institution agree to form a bargaining unit to rectify one or more of the following problems that they believe to exist:

Unsatisfactory representation in decisions affecting their future

Unfair selection and/or hiring procedures

Inadequate remuneration

Inadequate procedures for resolving grievances

Inadequate promotion and/or tenure processes

A general perception of mistreatment or neglect

Because the decision to establish a collective bargaining unit is normally based on a vote of the concerned employees, provisions for the treatment of a bargaining unit usually appear in personnel handbooks only after the decision has been made to bargain collectively. It would be extremely strange to find an institution making provision for dealing with a faculty bargaining unit in advance of a faculty demand for one. Hence, existing so-called *union security provisions* are usually based on multilateral bargaining on the conditions under which a unit can exist on campus. The specific terms of these agreements are likely to vary from one institution to another and from one bargaining situation to another.

In this chapter, we begin with a definition of the "appropriate bargaining unit," consider the issues that the creation of such a unit raises, and provide a sample agreement for an institution that deals with a union on campus. It should be obvious to our readers that the final shape of such an agreement, should their institution decide to write one, would depend on the nature of the bargaining between their institution and its bargaining unit.

An Appropriate Bargaining Unit for Full-Time Faculty

The issue of what is an appropriate bargaining unit for full-timers at an academic institution is an important one that defies easy resolution. Such a unit would include a group of employees with a *mutuality* or *community of interests* (i.e., with minimal *diversity of interests*). But what is mutuality in an academic context? Is it a common interest in the same subject matter (e.g., a department), a common interest in teaching (all faculty who teach), a common geographic location (all faculty in a city or institution), a common workload, or a common set of employment conditions? Anyone who has served on a university promotion and tenure or grievance committee has learned that the interests of full-time faculty are not always coincident at a modern academic institution. Sharp disciplinary differences distinguish the way that research is conducted, the amount of publication faculty are expected to do, the way consulting and public service are viewed, and even how scholarship is defined. What gives full-time faculty a common interest is the fact they are governed by a common set of policies and procedures, they service the same group of students, and they have a tradition of having worked together over many years.

Where a decentralized tradition of separate schools exists, an adversarial relationship is likely to develop among faculty. This might be the case, for example, when a law school develops its own unit for the purposes of bargaining collectively or when a medical school operates according to its own set of procedures. However, such situations are the exception rather than the rule. In general practice, most institutions have a common policy to govern their faculty, and this provides the basis for a similar set of concerns among members of the bargaining unit.

The Bargaining Unit Status of Part-Time Faculty

The issues with regard to the creation of a bargaining unit for part-time faculty and the definition of an appropriate bargaining unit have been primarily twofold in nature. The first involves whether part-timers should be included in a full-time bargaining unit if one already exists at their employing institution or whether part-timers should be included in education system-wide collective bargaining. The second involves whether they should be allowed to have a unit at all, and, if so, whether it can be a separate unit from the full-time unit. Since the precedents have been more extensively debated in the case of the first issue, we begin with this one, even though a more logical development would be to start with the second.

Whether part-time faculty should be included in a full-time bargaining unit has been both controversial and subject to various interpretations by legal entities over the years.[1] In 1973 the National Labor Relations Board (NLRB) stated in its *New York University* decision:

> After careful reflection, we have reached the conclusion that part-time faculty do not share a community of interest with full-time faculty and therefore should not be included in the same bargaining unit. . . . [The prime determinant for an ap-

> propriate bargaining unit is] mutuality of interest in wages, hours and working conditions.... In our judgment, the grouping of the part-time and full-time faculty into a single bargaining structure will impede effective collective bargaining.[2]

As demonstrable support for the mutuality of interest position, the NLRB excluded part-time faculty employed on a per-course basis from an appropriate bargaining unit consisting of both full-time faculty members and part-time faculty members having prorated full-time contracts.[3] Likewise, nuns of an order that owned and administered a college were excluded from a bargaining unit of lay faculty at that college.[4] However, in other circumstances when the NLRB excluded religious faculty from a faculty bargaining unit, its decisions were overruled as being arbitrary.[5]

Some state labor boards have included all part-time faculty in a unionized institution's appropriate bargaining unit. Specifically, state labor boards in California, Indiana, Massachusetts, Michigan, Montana, Oregon, Pennyslvania, Vermont, and Wisconsin have included part-time faculty as part of an appropriate bargaining unit for all faculty.[6] On these occasions, the state boards examined three of four elements cited in the *New York University* case previously referred to:

Faculty compensation

Faculty participation in university governance

Faculty working conditions

Faculty eligibility for tenure

The first three elements were regarded as important in clarifying the mutuality of interests between full- and part-time faculties in the nine states just mentioned. The final element, eligibility for tenure, was basically disregarded when defining appropriate bargaining unit. A precedent has been established, at least in those states, for part-time faculty to be included as part of the unit for collective bargaining purposes.

The second issue, whether part-timers should be allowed to have a unit at all, and, if so, whether it can be a separate unit was addressed in a NLRB decision in December 1982.[7] The situation involved a part-time faculty forming a distinct appropriate bargaining unit separate from that of full-tme faculty. In this case, the University of San Francisco Faculty Assocation sought to represent a unit of all part-time instructional faculty in a handful of schools within the university, as well as all part-time employees closely related academically. The University of San Franciso refused to recognize this unit, arguing that a unit of part-time faculty would be inappropriate because part-timers had temporary employment status.

The NLRB rejected the university's arguments, basing its decision on the fact that it failed to show part-time faculty were indeed temporary. It also ruled a community of interest existed among University of San Francisco part-time faculty, based on

1. The consistent method by which part-time faculty were hired and compensated

2. The standard university memorandum of employment that specified terms and conditions of employment for part-time faculty

3. The fact that part-time faculty could design their own curriculum and teaching methods within the bounds of course descriptions

4. The fact that part-time faculty were in contact with one another during the school year

5. The fact that part-time faculty worked similar hours

6. The fact that part-time faculty were subject to the same administrative structure

7. The fact that although the employer was not obligated to reappoint its part-time faculty members to teaching positions, it failed to show it did *not* offer its part-time faculty members reappointment

The issue of what is the appropriate composition of a bargaining unit is an important one. If part-time faculty are excluded from a bargaining unit because they are "temporary" employees, then they have no access to bargained agreements. This could potentially leave them open to arbitrary treatment, either by their employer or by the unit for full-timers. On the other hand, if part-time faculty are included in an appropriate bargaining unit, there exists a potential for an adversarial relationship between them and full-timers, since their interests do not correspond on a range of issues such as compensation, hiring, and governance. If full-time faculty outnumber their part-time faculty colleagues, a strong likelihood exists that part-timer interests will be overlooked. By the same token, in institutions where the number of part-timers exceeds that of full-timers, full-timers could conceivably find issues being resolved in a manner adverse to their best interests.[8]

The University of San Francisco case highlights another aspect of the problem. If one bargaining agent is strong and aggressive while the other is docile and passive, the employer may be forced to make allocation decisions based not on the best interests of the total faculty but rather on which group is stronger. In an environment like this, erosion of the concept of an academic institution as a *community* of scholars is almost inevitable, and the net losers will be those whom the institution serves. Whenever more than one agent represents the faculty, for whatever reason, the potential exists for adversarial issues to arise.

Are there any solutions, or at least hints of solutions, for the perplexed administrator about what position to take regarding the appropriate bargaining unit? As best as we can tell, the answer appears to be an unqualified "No." The type of bargaining unit(s) best suited to a particular institution that has voted to bargain collectively depends on a range of factors, including

Its past history with its employees

The fields and interests of its faculty

The form of contract it offers its part-timers

The form of compensation it offers its part-timers

The relationship between its part- and full-time faculty

Institutions seeking collective bargaining unit determinations should engage legal counsel about this subject. No omnibus sample policy statements on unit determination can be drafted that will cover the multitude of variables that come into play.

Union Security Policy Considerations

In designing a policy statement with regard to the institution's relationship with its union, it is important to bear in mind the following constraints:

1. The language included in the handbook should reflect the items agreed to in the union contract.

2. Specific items may be required to be included in the contract by the union's national organization.

3. Statements should not be included in the handbook until they have been agreed to by both parties. Failure to engage in prior consultation may lead to subsequent disagreements.

Here we provide sample statements concerning union security and dues check-off as illustrations for those unionized institutions that have not written handbooks for part-timers and for those about to become unionized. These sample statements assume compulsory union membership and compulsory dues checkoffs. It is emphasized that these statements would be appropriate only if the institution, as part of the collective bargaining process, agreed to compulsory union membership and compulsory dues checkoffs.

Sample Union Security Policy Statement

Part-time faculty covered by this agreement who, at the time it becomes effective, shall have been employed for 60 days or more and who are not members of the union shall be required as a condition of continued employment to become members of the union. Part-time faculty covered by this agreement who have been employed for less than 30 days when this agreement becomes effective shall be required as a condition of continued employment to become members of the union once they have been employed 30 days.

The union shall notify the institution and affected part-time faculty members in [the bargaining unit] who are 30 days in arrears in payment of membership dues. Part-time faculty members who fail to comply with the requirements of paying membership dues within 30 days of such notice shall be terminated from employment at the end of their current teaching assignment.

Sample Automatic Dues Check-Off Policy Statement

(Where Authorized in a Labor–Management Agreement) Part-time faculty members of [the bargaining unit] may authorize the institution automatically, to deduct from their pay the required amount of monthly union dues by filing with the payroll office [or other institutional organizational entity handling part-time pay matters] a written authorization. The dues and a list of part-time faculty members from whom the dues have been deducted along with the amount deducted shall be forwarded to the union mailing address no later than [usually 7 working days] after such deductions are made.

If dues are automatically deducted and remitted to the union as specified, the union shall be solely responsible for and agrees to indemnify and hold harmless the institution against any claims, demands, suits, or other forms of liability that may arise by reason of any action taken in making deductions and remitting them to the union.

Conclusions

There are no easy answers to the question of whether part-timers should be represented in a single bargaining unit with full-timers. The legal entities that have dealt with this question have provided conflicting answers, and recent collective bargaining agreements have failed to reflect a consensus position. It is our belief this issue is best left to the individual institution to resolve based on the criteria that we set forth.

The law is a little more definitive on the subject of whether part-timers may legitimately engage in bargaining. The fact they are transitory has not been judged to be grounds for their exclusion from the collective bargaining process. Hence, we would urge institutions faced with the question of whether or not to include part-timers in their bargaining process to give serious consideration to this possibility. Whether this should be done through a separate unit should be decided based on the criteria proposed in this chapter. It may well be true that in the next few years the courts will develop a common set of precedents in this area. At the moment, however, an institution facing the possibility of the formation of a collective bargaining unit that may include part-timers will have to be guided largely by a sense of what its own needs are and of the needs of its full- and part-timers.

Notes

1. Ronald B. Head, and David W. Leslie, "Bargaining Unit Status of Part-Time Faculty," *Journal of Law and Education* 8 (July 1979): 361–78.
2. 205 NLRB No. 16.
3. Kendall College (1978, CA7) 570 F2d 216.
4. Seton Hill College (1973) 201 NLRB 1026.
5. *Niagara University* v. *NLRB* (1977, CA2) 558 F2d 1116; *NLRB* v. *St. Francis College* (1977, CA3) 562 F2d 246.
6. Head and Leslie, "Bargaining Unit Status," p. 370.
7. *University of San Francisco* v. *NLRB* [265 NLRB No. 155 (1982)].
8. For an expanded treatment of part-time faculty inclusion or exclusion from bargaining units, see David W. Leslie, "Part-Time Faculty: Legal and Collective Bargaining Issues," *AAHE Bulletin,* (37)(October 1984): 8–12.

CHAPTER 12

The Integration into and Orientation of Part-Time Faculty to Their Employing Institution

The question of how continually to optimize the use of faculty resources is, and should be, a matter of concern for all academic institutions. Although colleges and universities are often thought of as ivory towers, in practice they are fairly pragmatic and very much aware of the social forces affecting them. Such forces require academic institutions to adjust to

Changes in the demand for particular courses and whole curricula

Changes in the composition of, and the services required by, the student body

Changes in the amount of and sources of revenue

Changes in the resource costs of production

Changes in the demand for the services provided to business, governmental entities, and the community

Changes in public and private funding for research

Changes in the number and types of competitors

Shortages in the supply of manpower in some fields

Surpluses of faculty in other fields

Because academic institutions are training grounds for society, they must be willing and able to respond to the trends enumerated above in order to survive. But many aspects of the academic environment make it difficult for such changes to occur with rapidity. At least four aspects of the academic environment make flexible response difficult:

1. *The human element.* Faculty and staff are usually resistant to change. They must be prepared for change and convinced that any changes they make will not adversely affect them. This can be a slow process.

2. *Tenure rules.* Tenure precludes easy movement of full-time faculty from one curriculum to another. Tenure decisions made in the 1960s affect an institution's ability to shift resources well into the 1990s.

3. *Limited information.* Most institutions are unable to determine what is a temporary trend and what is permanent. This causes them to move slowly and cautiously in responding to a changing environment.

4. *The regulatory environment.* Particularly at public institutions, extensive rules and regulations govern what can and cannot be done to move funds from one account to another or to shift positions from one unit to another. All institutions face publicly imposed rules governing recruitment of students, hiring of faculty, granting of aid, recruitment for sports programs, and other restrictions on resource management. This makes it difficult for them to respond in the way that they wish to.

To counteract these constraints, academic institutions must

seek ways to increase their flexibilty. Part-timers provide a useful solution when staffing problems arise, because they can staff courses for which demand has temporarily risen, cover courses in which a shortage of faculty has occurred, help to reduce manpower costs, and provide a quick response to changing curriculum demands. But part-timers can also prove to be a liability to their employing organization if they are not properly integrated into the teaching faculty. Because many institutions assume that part-timers are short-term employees, they send them into the classroom with little or no prior orientation. This is unfortunate since it can reduce part-timer productivity and thus deny an institution the full benefits that it might obtain from the use of part-timers.

Academic institutions need clear policy statements of how part-time faculty are to be integrated into their program. Such statements will serve not only to orient part-timers to their role in the organization but also as a guide to full-timers as well. A well-articulated policy avoids misunderstandings between part-timers and their employers and provides a set of guidelines to the persons who ultimately hire them.

In this chapter, we attempt to stimulate serious thinking as to the appropriate policies that an institution should adopt. The following sections illustrate the issues that need to be addressed in integrating part-time faculty into an academic institution and in orienting them to their environment. The policies proposed are designed to be representational, not exhaustive.

Limits on Part-Time Hiring

A prime concern among academic planners involves the issue of whether to limit the number of part-timers employed at an institution. It is not our desire to take a position on this issue since it involves considerations best addressed on a case-by-case basis. However, if an academic institution wishes to impose a numerical limit on the usage of part-time faculty, it is our belief that its policies should be spelled out explicity. The fundamental issues involve (1) how many positions part-timers will be allowed to hold, either absolutely or relative to full-timers (also expressed as how much of the course load they should be allowed to carry), and (2) whether part-timers will be hired only after the full-timers in a department have received their course assignments.

The former issue is addressed through the imposition of specific numerical limits on hires. These may be absolute or relative. For example, a statement such as "One part-time faculty member per discipline per division is permitted" can be a useful planning and control tool; or "It shall be the policy of this institution to hire no more than one part-timer for every five full-time faculty members in a discipline or division." Such statements permit decentralization of hiring within predetermined guidelines. They also clarify the rules of the game for those responsible for hiring part-timers.

Alternatively, academic institutions may wish to limit part-time faculty teaching loads to a specific number of hours: for example, "No more than 10 credit hours per semester may be taught by part-timers in a single department. Any department chair who wishes to utilize part-timers to teach in excess of these hours should request specific permission from the dean." The limitation may also be expressed as a percentage of the standard full-time teaching load: for example, "Part-time faculty may teach up to a maximum of 50% of the regular full-time faculty teaching load in a department."

If an institution's policy is not to place limits on the use of part-timers, this should also be explicitly spelled out: "No limits are placed on the number of part-timers employed by a department. Instead, a determination of the need for part-time hires is made based on student enrollments, the number of full-time faculty available for assignment, the types of skills required of faculty, and the times at which courses are scheduled. The total number of part-timers will be arrived at by the dean in consultation with the department chair."

The second policy issue, whether part-timers should be hired before all full-timers have been used, should also be addressed specifically: for example, "Departments may hire a part-time faculty member only when all full-time faculty have been assigned to a full-time load." This statement aids deans and department chairs in planning and controlling the use of part-time faculty members; alternatively, "Departments may hire up to three part-time faculty without prior consultation with the dean provided that there are at least 30 students enrolled in the classes that they are assigned to teach." A policy statement that permits departments to hire part-time faculty members only after all full-time faculty have been assigned *and* offered a chance to teach an overload course may help reduce opposition to using part-timers. Most institutions will wish to recognize the case where a part-timer has a special skill not available among full-time faculty. In this instance, the language will need to be modified such as, for example, "Qualified part-time faculty with special skills or specific expertise not possessed by members of the full-time faculty will be employed to teach courses requiring such skills or expertise even if all full-time faculty are not fully assigned."

An academic institution may also specifically recognize the hiring of part-time faculty to substitute for full-time faculty on sabbatical leave or engaged in nonteaching activities. Such persons may either be exempted from, or included in, the numerical limits set above: "Part-timers hired to substitute for faculty on sabbatical leave, or those engaged in nonteaching activities, shall be excluded from the numerical limits set forth above."

This discussion makes clear that the formulation of a set of policies governing the use of part-timers involves a fair amount of discussion and debate. There are no easy answers to the question of how many part-timers an institution ought to hire. The ultimate resolution is likely to rest on a consensus position.

Part-Time Faculty Orientation and Development

This section addresses the question of how part-time faculty should be integrated into the academic environment. It also touches upon part-time faculty professional development. Studies of part-timers who have employment other than that at their surveyed institution typically reveal that they

Often have other full-time jobs

Have less teaching experience than full-time faculty

Have a primary allegiance to their full-time job

Prepare less for class than full-time faculty

Have less contact time with students than do full-timers

Feel a sense of separation from the full-time faculty

Often are not acquainted with the basic teaching- and discipline-oriented philosophies of their employing institution

Often have special skills not available among full-time faculty

May also be teachers at other institutions

Are often very committed to their part-time faculty positions[1]

These findings suggest that academic insitutions might benefit from clear-cut orientation programs specifically tailored to the needs of part-time faculty. While it may seem self-evident that academic administrators would wish to integrate part-timers into their program by orienting them and providing developmental opportunities, the following quotation from a 1980 study shows that this is not necessarily true:

> Part-time faculty [orientation and] development seems to be viewed as a poor investment of critical dollars. . . . While this may smack of exploitation, it is a realistic assessment of what is presently working.[2]

Moreover, part-timers are often isolated from the academic mainstream of their disciplines, departments, and institutions. Another study of part-timers concludes:

> [Part-time faculty] were less likely to teach courses on campus and had less than complete support from such services as the bookstore, the library, media center, student personnel, duplication, and secretarial staff.[3]

To mitigate such isolation and better integrate part-time faculty, administrators might capitalize on part-timer uniqueness. For example, part-time faculty with other jobs are particularly likely to have strong links to their communities. These part-timers could be asked to assist students in finding positions after graduation. The expectation that they would help might foster in part-timers a sense of belonging and institutional identity. Another tactic that might be employed without undue difficulty would be to have part-timers assist full-timers in obtaining research grants or consulting projects. Such activities would form constructive linkages between the two groups.

Reciprocal requests might be made of full-timers. For example, each part-timer might be assigned a full-time person to contact in the event that problems arise. Part-timers might also be invited to visit at least one full-timer-taught class to see how the material is approached and to gain a grounding in the departmental philosophy (or lack thereof). They might also be asked to attend an occasional faculty meeting to become known to full-timers. At a minimum, they should be notified as to when department meetings are held and sent a copy of the minutes. Policies such as these help to create a greater sense of participation and of identity with the employing institution.

Specific information that may be included in an orientation program for integrating part-time faculty into academic life is outlined in the following paragraphs. This is intended as a catalyst to stimulate thinking and further work by our readers.

Orientation and Professional Development of Part-Time Faculty Members

To ensure that newly appointed part-time faculty members are adequately informed about philosophies, policies, practices, and procedures, academic institutions should thoroughly orient and provide development opportunities for these people. To aid them in offering an effective orientation and development program, we have listed items that might be included in such a program and a manual.[4]

Recommended List of Items to Be Included in Part-Time Faculty Orientation

I. Introduction
- State the philosophy and objectives of the institution and how they relate to the part-timer's role.
- State the role of the institution in the community.

II. Administrative Information
- Clarify who will serve as administrative contact with the institution.
- Specify who in the institution is responsible for what functions. Provide a list of administrative units and their key people.
- State when and where academic materials such as syllabi, course outlines, reproduction work, etc., must be submitted.
- State the conditions of employment.
- State the pay periods and deductions.
- Clarify what the part-time faculty member is supposed to do when he or she cannot make a class.
- Specify the kinds of administrative support (e.g., secretarial assistance, office space, parking, and materials duplication) the part-time faculty member can expect to receive.
- Clarify who evaluates the part-time faculty member, along with how this should be done.
- Specify roll-keeping requirements.
- Specify institutional policies regarding classroom breaks.
- Specify where the part-time faculty member should obtain supplies such as chalk, slides, test booklets, etc.
- Clarify who the part-time faculty member should see to get answers to questions.
- Clarify the part-timer's teaching responsibilities (review Chapter 8 for a sample statement of teacher responsibilities).
- Provide the part-time faculty member with a general job description (one is provided in Chapter 8).

- Specify how a part-time faculty member can get classroom and building doors unlocked.
- Provide a school calendar (include social activities and pay days).
- Clarify how the part-time faculty members should handle drops and adds.
- Specify when classes start and end.
- Specify what the institution's student attendance policy is.
- Specify procedures for turning in grades.
- Provide a list of full-time faculty.
- Provide a list of institutional parking regulations.
- Provide a list of standing faculty committees.
- Provide information on policies and procedures regarding audiovisual equipment.
- Ensure that part-time faculty know the procedures for admitting late-registering students into classes.
- Ensure that part-time faculty know the policies for canceling classes because of bad weather.

Note: Frequently used forms and complete instructions for their use should be included in the handbook. Telephone lists, office addresses (especially those of the various chairpersons), supportive services, catalogues, and campus maps would also be useful to include.

III. Academic Information
- Provide information about who, if anyone, will assist the part-time faculty member with teaching techniques.
- Include information about teaching evaluation procedures.
- Provide hints about how to arrange for guest lectures and field trips.
- Clarify questions about part-time faculty office hours and space to conduct student conferences.
- Provide information about how to provide students with tutorial assistance.
- Provide tips on specific tasks that need to be completed during the first class (a checklist would be helpful).

- Clarify procedures for the part-time faculty member to contact a student at home or work.
- Clarify procedures as to how to obtain information about the background of students.
- Ensure the part-time faculty member knows institutional policies about grading and the system for turning in grades.
- Specify procedures to be followed if the part-time faculty member catches a student cheating.
- Give the part-time faculty member detailed information on library resources and ways to reserve books in the library for the short and long term.

IV. Emergency Procedures
- Provide information on how to reach campus security and campus medical facilities. Ensure that the part-time faculty member knows the procedures for obtaining emergency assistance.
- Provide a list of emergency telephone numbers.

If all these items are touched upon in an orientation program and included in a part-time faculty staff manual, solid lines of communication will have been opened between the institution and its part-time faculty. This is a healthy, constructive step in helping part-timers to develop into supportive institutional employees.

Conclusions

Good lines of communication do not develop between the employees of an organization and its administrators automatically. Steps must be taken to orient employees to their hiring institution. This involves providing background on the nature and philosophy of the institution, what it has to offer its employees, its physical plant, and its services. Such orientation takes time and effort to prepare and present, but it can pay off in terms of future dividends in the form of increased productivity, greater employee satisfaction on the job, and greater institutional identification and loyalty. Some of the policies that an institution has toward its part-timers are likely to be controversial, particularly those involving how many part-timers should be hired. These policies should be promulgated only after taking into account all the factors that bear on the institution in question. The faculty handbook should be as explicit as possible in laying out policies relevant to the orientation and integration of part-timers to their employer institution. A detailed example of such a handbook is provided in the Appendix.

Notes

1. See Margaret Haddad and Mary Ellen Dickens, "Competencies for Part-Time Faculty—The First Step," *Community and Junior College Journal,* 49 (November 1978): 22–24.
2. Alan John Schreibmeier, "An Investigation of Part-Time Faculty Staff Development in Public Community Junior Colleges in the United States," Ph.D. dissertation, University of Texas at Austin, 1980.
3. Ronald Hoenninger and Richard A. Black, "Neglect of a Species," *Community and Junior College Journal,* 49 (November 1978): 25–27.
4. This list is adapted from one provided to the authors by Dr. Mary Ellen Duncan, Director, Eastern Regional Center, National Technical Assistance Consortium for Two-Year Colleges, Tri-County Technical College, P.O. Box 587, Pendleton, SC 29670.

Appendix:
Essential Elements of a Part-Time Faculty Handbook

This Appendix brings together the essentials of a part-time faculty handbook in one place. It begins with the assumption that an academic institution needs to base a part-time faculty manual on a wide variety of considerations including

- Governance constraints
- Budgetary limitations
- Type of governance (public–private)
- Level of instruction (2-year, 4-year, etc.)
- Unionized or nonunionized status
- Availability of qualified part- and full-time faculty
- Institutional philosophy on faculty selection
- Institutional philosophy on faculty evaluation

The essential elements of a part-time faculty handbook are presented below. Our intent is to provide a model that can be

135

modified to reflect the considerations listed above. On some topics actual policy statements are provided, while on others the reader is referred to other parts of the book for sample language. The handbook is divided into three sections: *Section I* is based on the assumption that a handbook will begin with an overview section. This contains an introduction to the academic institution designed to orient the part-timer to the cultural and institutional environment of his or her employing institution. *Section II* addresses the specific contractual matters and the performance expectations that need to be clarified and agreed to by both the institution and the part-timers it employs. *Section III* discusses the administrative issues that should be resolved to enable the part-timer to function effectively as a member of the employing institution.

Our sample handbook is intended as a departure point. We do not envision, nor do we recommend, the wholesale lifting of the text as the sole basis for a part-time faculty handbook. Each institution has its own unique needs, and only by a careful thinking through of the issues from the point of view of the considerations raised above can an institution arrive at a set of policies and procedures right for its environment. The following guideposts are not a substitute for the process of thinking through the issues in defining an integrated policy toward the employment of part-timers. It is the process itself that produces an institutional consensus on the role of part-timers.

SAMPLE PART-TIME FACULTY HANDBOOK

Section I: Introduction to the Institution

HISTORY OF THE INSTITUTION

In this section, a brief institutional history is provided to the part-time faculty member.

ACCREDITATION STANDARDS

Presented here are the accreditation standards applicable to the institution.

BOARD OF TRUSTEES (REGENTS)

A brief description of the relevant institutional governance policies is provided.

INSTITUTIONAL ADMINISTRATIVE ORGANIZATION

A thumbnail sketch of the institution's administrative organization and its formal chains of command is presented.

INSTITUTIONAL ENVIRONMENT

A statement of the philosophy, mission, role, and other aspects of the institutional environment is provided. Such issues are discussed as the type of commitment to education (e.g., educate the top versus the middle), effect of residential or nonresidential status, whether the institution is inexpensive or expensive and selective or nonselective, attitudes toward teaching, and values the insitution seeks to inculcate. The purpose of this section is to describe and define the institution's role in the community and its approach toward higher education.

STUDENT POPULATION

This section describes the student body and provides demographic information about these students that will help the part-timer to understand who he or she is teaching.

Section II: Part-Time Faculty Contractual Matters

INSTITUTIONAL PHILOSOPHY TOWARD THE USE OF PART-TIME FACULTY MEMBERS

A statement of why part-time faculty members are hired at this intitution is provided. The following statement uses brackets to highlight alternative forms of wording that depend on the particular policy options selected.

This institution employs temporary part-time faculty members whose skills and teaching abilities qualify them as effective teachers for the following reasons:

1. Part-timers provide a flow of ideas from the world of work to the classroom.

2. Part-timers are used to offer special courses, technology, or programs that do not attract enough students to warrant a full-time instructor.

3. Part-time faculty are used to offer courses scheduled at a location and/or time when full-time faculty are unavailable to teach them.

4. Part-timers are used to test new courses and programs and to build course offerings in curricula with limited numbers of students.

5. Part-timers are used to adapt to fluctuating enrollments, either in particular programs or across the institution.

6. Part-time employment is offered to persons with unique skills who either could not be paid enough on a full-time basis to come to the institution or whose skills are in such short supply that they could not be obtained on a full-time basis.

In short, the use of part-time faculty enables this institution to enrich its classroom teaching, ensure that contemporary practice and classroom teaching are in consonance, build bridges to the local community, and be flexible toward unexpected social and economic changes.

Most persons employed as part-time faculty will have another source of income that is the primary one. Their income from part-time employment will be supplemental to the levels needed for maintenance of a reasonable standard of living. [For those dependent on part-time teaching for a living, arrangements will be made to help insure adequate coverage for health and retirement benefits.]

Because this institution has a complex selection process for full-time faculty, it is understood that a part-time teaching assignment is not intended as an entry into regular employment unless this institution has specified in writing that the part-timer is in a tenure-track position. [Part-timers who work at this institution for more than 3 years shall be considered eligible for assignment to a part-time tenure-track position.] [Part-timers who meet the standards for hire of a full-time faculty member may apply for a full-time position as a full-time faculty member at this institution after a period of 3 years. Their previous experience as part-timers shall not give them priority in the selection process.]

Part-time faculty are expected to possess credentials acceptable to their department of hire. [Part-timers are expected to have levels of excellence in training, education, experience, and performance equal to those of the full-timers employed in their department of hire.]

Part-time faculty are not expected to participate [or participate at the same level of commitment] in committee and other governance activities. The difference in their workload is a principal reason for the lower rate of compensation they receive relative to full-time faculty. [Part-timers working more than half of a full-time load may be asked to engage in governance activities and, if they do, shall be compensated to reflect their additional workload.]

EQUAL EMPLOYMENT OPPORTUNITY

A statement about the institution's commitment to equal employment opportunities for all part-time faculty members, irrespective of their race, color, religion, sex, national origin, age, pregnancy status, handicaps or Viet Nam veteran's status is provided.

This institution adheres to a policy of offering equal employment opportunity to all who apply irrespective of race, color, religion, age, sex, national origin, age, pregnancy status, handicapped status, or Vietnam veteran status. [The institution may wish to enumerate its equal employment opportunity and affirmative action policies here.]

TYPE OF CONTRACT

The type of part-time faculty contract an institution uses should be based on the part-timer's workload, attachment to the institution, specialty, and value. It will also depend on past practice. If an institution has a unionized full-time or part-time faculty, the union's security policy statement should be included here. The reader is referred to the sample union security policy statement in Chapter 11.

PART-TIME FACULTY TEACHING RESPONSIBILITIES

The teaching responsibilities of part-time faculty should be clearly articulated here. The sample statement presented in Chapter 8 is reproduced below.

Sample Statement of Part-Time Faculty Teaching Responsibilities

The responsibilities of part-time faculty are as follow:

1. The assigned classes in a specified specialty should be conducted in accordance with the catalogue description and the stipulations of the institution.

2. Behavioral learning objectives should be developed for each course. A behavioral learning objective specifies the changes in student behavior expected as a result of taking the course. A model for writing behavioral learning objectives is as follows:

   By the end of this course, the student should be able to [demonstrate some *performance*] [measured by some *criterion*] [under some *condition*]. An example is: By the end of this course, the student should be able to write a complex BASIC computer program that is operational without referring to a reference text.

3. Every class, including the final examination, should be held the full scheduled number of minutes in the assigned classroom. Every scheduled class should be met and taught, even if this is inconvenient. Classes will be canceled only as a last resort. Whenever a part-time faculty member is to be absent, he or she must notify the immediate academic supervisor. Missed classes must be made up. Various levels of "coverage" in order of preference are

- [The class meets and is taught, or the examination is given, so that the syllabus is carried forward in spite of the absence. This should be especially possible in multisection courses where different instructors and sections can be assumed to be fairly well together in a generally common syllabus.]

- [The class meets and is continued throughout the period by discussion, review, in-class written assignment, or similar instructional technique.]

- [The class meets, roll is taken, and the class is then dismissed for further research or other written work previously assigned.]

- [The class is canceled.]

Each part-time faculty member is authorized one [paid or unpaid, depending upon institutional preference—it is suggested this be *paid*] absence per semester, on a noncumulative basis, as the result of illness. Such an absence is defined as one that occurs on any 1 calendar day, during either a regular semester or a summer term, on which the part-time faculty member is scheduled to teach. For absences not attributable to illness or for absences involving more than 1 calendar day per semester and attributable to illness, the responsibility for financial arrangements for a guest instructor rests with the part-time faculty member.

4. Standards of teaching that are worthy of accreditation must be maintained.

5. Means of improving instruction should be sought out through professional meetings, societies, workshops, and the current literature of the field. Aid and assistance in these matters may be obtained from colleagues, department chairpersons, program coordinators, academic supervisors, and learning resource personnel.

6. Insofar as possible, teaching methods should be adjusted to student needs.

7. Mid-term and final grade reports must be submitted *on time*.

8. A copy of the final examination and syllabus, reading lists, and other instructional materials of like nature should be submitted to the appropriate academic supervisor.

9. Faculty must be available for student consultation for each course taught in accordance with institutional guidelines.

DEFINITION OF WHO IS A FACULTY MEMBER

This section provides definitions of all faculty categories. For full-time faculty, this include all ranks (e.g., full, associate, and assistant professor and instructor) along with the specific requirements for hiring, selection, evaluation, and promotion to each level. These materials should replicate the statements provided in the policy manual to full-time faculty.

Following these descriptions, part-time faculty ranks would be outlined. The statements in Chapter 4 are reproduced here.

The [campus authority designated to do this—usually the provost] authorizes initial placement of part-time faculty into the entry-, middle-, or senior-level ranks. Rank and salary are determined by giving credit for each year of past college teaching (either part-time or fulltime), and for other appropriate educational experience and up to one-half year for each year of related experience. The general guidelines the [campus authority] uses for determining seniority and thereby rank and salary are as follow:

1. One year of full-time service in teaching at the [university, college, or 2-year college, as appropriate] level is equivalent to 1 year of experience for rank and salary determination.

2. Eighteen semester hours of part-time faculty teaching experience are equivalent to 1 year of experience for rank and salary determination.

3. Each 2 years of related educational (elementary or secondary school teaching), industrial, or research experience may be equated to 1 year of experience for rank and salary determination, depending upon the degree of relevance of the experience to the teaching assignment.

SELECTION AS A PART-TIME FACULTY MEMBER

In this section, personnel policies for appointment to the part-time faculty are clearly presented. All matters pertaining to selection criteria, application forms, interviews, supervisory review, and other personnel selection procedures are addressed here. Documentation requirements expected of any new employee are also spelled out.

Qualifications For Selection as a Part-Time Faculty Member

Entry Level: To qualify for appointment to an *entry-level* part-time position, a candidate should have academic *or* professional experience comparable with that required for appointment to the full-time rank of instructor. *Academically,* a candidate should have made substantial progress toward the doctorate, if a doctorate is considered customary in his or her discipline. *Experientially,* a candidate should have an employment history relevant to his or her teaching field and of sufficient duration to satisfy the requirements of the course(s) being taught.

Middle Level: To qualify for appointment to a *Middle-Level* part-time faculty position, a candidate should have academic *or* professional experience comparable with that for appointment to the full-time rank of either assistant or associate professor. *Academically,* an appointee to this rank should hold the doctorate, if customary in his or her discipline. *Experientially,* relevant full-time responsibility and achievement need to be shown. Additionally, a candidate should have demonstrated capability for further professional growth in his or her field.

Senior Level: To qualify for appointment to a *senior-level* part-time faculty position, a candidate should have academic *or* professional experience comparable with that of a full-time professor. Additionally, the equivalent of 10 years of teaching experience should have been attained with commendable ratings from students and other persons who have had an opportunity to observe teaching styles. *Academically,* a doctorate should have been earned, if customary within the discipline. Contributions to the scholarship of the field should have been made. *Experientially,* a candidate must have had relevant full-time professional responsibility, significant achievement, and an impressive standing in his or her professional field.

DOCUMENTATION REQUIREMENTS

The following documentation is required:

- A current resumé or curriculum vitae that includes pertinent information on which to base an appointment decision, such as degrees received, teaching experience, and professional affiliations

- An endorsement from the administrator recommending the appointment

- Student teaching evaluations if available

- Publications, if any, in a field pertinent to the course subject matter

- Valid academic transcripts from their colleges and universities

APPOINTMENT DOCUMENTATION

Statements regarding required documentation for part-time faculty appointments are included in this section. Because of varying requirements for initial appointments that are imposed by different institutions, review of Chapter 4 is encouraged prior to creating a tailored policy statement on this topic.

A member of the adjunct faculty is appointed for a period of up to 2 years. The appointment must be considered for official renewal at the completion of this appointment period. Renewal can occur only after an analysis of course load requirements for the ensuing appointment period has been made, verification of satisfactory teaching evaluations has been completed, and a review of the part-time faculty member's academic and professional progress over the previous appointment period has been undertaken. Where a decision is made to renew the part-time faculty member's contract, a formal contract must be renegotiated with the faculty member for the ensuing 2-year period. A part-time faculty member will be compensated only for sessions during which he or she has specified contractual duties and for which specific services have been rendered.

The [campus authority designated to do this—usually the provost] authorizes initial placement of part-time faculty into the entry-, middle-, or senior-level ranks. Rank and salary placement is determined by giving credit for each year of past college teaching or other appropriate educational experience and up to one-half year for each year of related experience. General guidelines the [campus authority] would use for determining seniority and thereby both rank and salary placement are as follow:

1. One year of full-time service in teaching at the [university, college, or 2-year college, as appropriate] level is equivalent to 1 year of experience for rank and salary determination.
2. Eighteen semester hours of part-time faculty teaching experience are equivalent to 1 year of experience for rank and salary determination.
3. Each 2 years of related educational (elementary or secondary school teaching), industrial, or research experience may be equated to 1 year of experience for rank and salary determination, depending upon the relevance of the experience to the materials being taught.

EVALUATION CRITERIA

Statements regarding evaluation criteria are included in this section. An institution can have a variety of evaluation techniques, including student ratings, peer evalutions, and supervisory ratings. The procedures for and use of evaluations should be clearly spelled out here. A sample statement for the evaluation of part-time faculty was provided in Chapter 9 and this is is reproduced here. These are based upon differing levels of part-time faculty utilization.

1. Part-time faculty shall be evaluated at least once during the academic year. New part-time faculty shall be evaluated within 6 weeks of their initial contract.
2. Part-timers shall be evaluated by appropriate student groups and by the teaching unit supervisor.

3. Times and dates for the evaluation procedures will be promulgated in advance.
4. The teaching unit supervisor shall review the evaluation with the part-time faculty member. The results of the evaluation will be filed in the part-timer's official personnel folder.
5. Part-time faculty will be evaluated using the same evaluation instruments as are used for full-time faculty members.
6. The variables used in evaluating a part-time faculty member should include at least the following:
    a. Complexity of the course
    b. Whether the course is optional or required in an academic degree program
    c. Number of students in the class
    d. Whether the course is specifically designed to service adult or traditional students

CRITERIA FOR PROMOTION

Promotion criteria are necessary if the institution employs long-term part-timers. Each criterion should be spelled out in sufficient detail so that part-time faculty know exactly what institutional expectations are. Likewise, they should be specific enough that administrators can point to reasonable, measurable achievements as the basis for promotion. Such criteria are best left to each institution to develop, based upon its evaluation criteria and types of contracts. Chapter 9 discusses the components of part-time faculty evaluation and promotion systms.

GRIEVANCE PROCEDURES

Several alternative grievance procedures can be used for part-timers, and these are discussed in Chapter 10. Because of its length, the statement provided in that chapter is not reproduced here.

SEPARATION, LAYOFF, DISCHARGE FOR CAUSE

An academic institution has the right to terminate a part-time faculty member because of an absence of sufficient class enrollments to warrant this employment, economic exigencies, or other justifiable causes. A statement of causes as well as of other bases for discharge should be included here.

ACADEMIC FREEDOM

Academic freedom to explore controversial issues and topics should be extended to all instructional staff including part-time faculty.

Academic freedom includes the right to express oneself responsibly without fear of retribution based on any characteristic such as sex. An institutional policy statement mandating equal opportunity for employment and proscribing sexual harassment would be appropriate here.

FACULTY DEVELOPMENT

Faculty development was addressed in Chapter 12. Items relevant to how individuals can develop themselves and how the institution encourages development can be inserted here.

FRINGE BENEFITS

A discussion of fringe benefits was provided in Chapter 6. Depending upon the level of benefits offered to part-time faculty, a policy statement should be placed here indicating which benefits are offered to part-time faculty as part of their employment contract and which are available on an optional basis. The institution should also make explicit its intent to treat part-time faculty fairly relative to full-timers.

SALARY RATIONALE

A discussion of part-time faculty salaries was provided in Chapter 5. The institutional rationale for the setting of part-time faculty compensation should be placed in a handbook. If salary is based on a prorated amount of full-time faculty salary or on some other procedure discussed in Chapter 5, this information should be provided here.

TENURED STATUS

Part-time faculty considered qualified for placement in a tenure-track position are provided the appropriate criteria for tenure in this section. A sample policy statement gleaned from information provided to the reader in Chapter 7 is offered. If this policy statement does not fit an institution's requirements, the reader is referred to Chapter 7.

1. Part-time service at less than one-half time shall not be counted in the probationary period of a tenure-track part-time faculty member. Each year of service at the rate of at least one-half time but no more than three-quarters time shall count as one-half of a year for probationary purposes. Services at a rate greater than three-quarters time shall be counted as a full year. In no case shall the probationary period exceed [a reasonable time frame is 12 years].

2. In all respects other than length of probationary period, standards of teaching performance and scholarly endeavor shall be the same for full-time and part-time faculty.

3. If tenure is ultimately recommended by the teaching unit, the part-time faculty member will receive a prorata appointment with tenure, i.e., one-half, three-quarters, two-thirds, etc., of regular full-time appointment.

Section III: Administrative Matters

AUDIOVISUAL AIDS

The institutional procedures for checking out and using audiovisual aids should be stated. Include phone numbers and accountability and other pertinent information. If there are forms to fill out, include a sample form in this section.

AUDIT PROCEDURES

Procedures for students to audit a class should be described and institutional requirements for auditors included.

BASIS FOR REWARDING CREDIT

The institutional requirements for awarding credit for courses enrolled in and completed should be specified.

CAMPUS VISITORS

If there are any restrictions on visitors coming onto the campus, they should be provided in this section.

CHEATING AND PLAGIARISM

A statement similar to the following is useful in this section of the handbook:

All students are expected to achieve their goals with academic honesty. Cheating and plagiarism are not tolerated. If cheating or plagiarism are observed or detected, the part-time faculty member should notify the student that evidence of the offense will be turned over to the department chairperson for resolution.

CLASS ADMISSION

Institutional policies on admitting students into a class who are not on an official roster should be spelled out for the part-time faculty member. Forms used to add–drop the course should also be included here.

CLASS ASSIGNMENT

How rooms are assigned, who to see about getting rooms changed, and other pertinent information should be presented here.

CLASS ATTENDANCE

A sample statement that might apply to all institutions is as follows:

It is the belief of this institution that regular and prompt attendance is essential to scholastic success and growth. Students are expected to attend all scheduled classes and examinations except in cases of emergency. If for some reason a student is absent from class, the number of absences should not exceed the number of semester hours of credit for the course. This provision for class "cuts" is not an encouragement to miss class but rather a way to allow students to make up work missed when absent from class because of illness or other unexpected situations that may arise.

The effect of absences on grades is determined by the instructor. If any student accumulates more absences than allowed, the student will be referred to a higher authority in the institution. Excessive absences from class may result in the student being dropped from the course.

CLASS LENGTH

Information about how long each class is, along with specific information concerning breaks, tardiness, etc., should be included in this section.

CLASS SCHEDULING

How classes are scheduled, who is responsible for assigning sections, and how course offerings are made are of interest to part-time faculty members and should be provided here.

CLERICAL SERVICES

Part-time faculty often are expected to provide their own clerical and reproduction services. This is inequitable. Institutions should provide clerical and reproduction services to faculty. Details on how to arrange for typing, reproduction, makeup examinations, proctoring, etc., should be supplied.

CLOSED CLASS

Part-time faculty should be advised on how to turn away persons wishing to enroll when a class has attained its maximum enrollment.

Since this can be awkward, it is recommended that the part-time faculty have the student see the department chairperson or another administrative individual to explain the institutional policies on closed classes.

CONFERENCE AREAS

Many institutions are unable to provide part-time faculty with either an office or dedicated space to conduct private conferences or office hours. When the institution can provide this type of facility, details should be provided in this section of the handbook.

COPYRIGHT LAW

A statement such as the following is considered appropriate for adherence to copyright policies:

In producing material originated by others, individuals must be careful not to infringe on the rights of the originator, which are protected by copyright laws. In this regard, as a minimum, it is necessary that all part-time faculty

- Read carefully and comply with the copyright statement contained in the material

- Obtain permission for reproduction from the author or publisher, where such is required, prior to duplication in whole or in part

- Quote, footnote, or otherwise give due credit where verbatim extracts are made

- Footnote and give due credit where concepts are borrowed substantively from a copyrighted document

- Arrange, where required, to pay royalties for the use of copyrighted material

COURSE OUTLINE, GOALS, AND OBJECTIVES

A statement similar to the following is useful in this section of the handbook:

Every part-time faculty member is expected to prepare goals, objectives, and an outline for each course taught. (Note: For further guidance on how to prepare behavioral objectives, see the materials in Chapter 8.) During the first week of class, the part-time faculty member is expected to inform students of the goals and objectives of the course and the means of determining grades.

COURSE RECORDS

A statement similar to the following is useful in this section of the handbook:

The part-time faculty member is expected to maintain an accurate record of how students' grades are determined. Should attendance be used as an aspect of student performance, accurate attendance records must also be kept.

CURRICULUM PLANNING

The institution needs to determine the extent to which part-time faculty will be used to plan course content and substance. A statement that clarifies the institution's expectations for part-time faculty member's participation in the curriculum-planning process is appropriate for insertion here.

CUSTODIAL SERVICES

When the institution has procedures for providing special custodial and cleanup services, this information should be offered here.

DEAN'S LIST INFORMATION

A statement similar to the following is useful in this section of the handbook:

At the end of the semester, the dean's list is published to honor those students who have a semester–quarter–trimester [whichever is applicable] grade point average of _____ or higher.

EMERGENCY PROCEDURES

A statement similar to the following is useful in this section of the handbook:

Should a student become seriously ill or injured on campus, part-time faculty members should use the following emergency procedures:

- Call [the appropriate number].

- Notify a member of the administrative staff of the emergency [provide the name and number of a contact point if one is used at the institution]. If no one is available, call the switchboard operator and relay the details of the emergency to him or her.

- Accompany or ensure that a staff member accompanies the injured–ill person to the emergency room.

EXAMINATIONS

A statement similar to the following is useful in this section of the handbook:

This institution considers examinations to be part of the learning process, and the experience has been that frequent examinations are preferable to only one examination. Therefore, faculty are encouraged to schedule examinations on a regular basis. Every effort should be made to provide students with prompt feedback regarding the examination results. During the time allotted for the final examination, faculty are required to give an examination or schedule some equally appropriate educational activity.

FIRE DRILLS

If there are any institutional procedures for fire drills, they should be specified in this section.

GRADE APPEAL PROCEDURES

Some institutions have specific administrative procedures appealing grades. These procedures should be included here.

GRADE CHANGE

Procedures for changing of grades should be specified.

GRADE SYSTEM AND REPORTING

Detailed descriptions of grading practices and procedures should be specified here. Unique requirements, such as the requirement to have a minimum of a 2.0 grade point average in every major course, should also be included in this section.

IDENTIFICATION CARD

If the institution requires an identification card, this information should be included here, along with the procedures for obtaining and updating one.

INCLEMENT WEATHER PROCEDURES

Procedures for canceling classes in inclement weather should be included here.

INDEPENDENT STUDIES

If part-time faculty are permitted to monitor independent studies, the procedures for doing so should be included here.

JOB OR POSITION DESCRIPTION

Job or position descriptions were discussed in Chapter 8. The reader is referred to Chapter 8 for a sample part-time faculty job description.

KEYS

Policies on obtaining room keys should be written here.

LIBRARY RESOURCES

All information concerning using institutional library resources should be supplied in this section. This includes requests for book resources, regulations of part-time faculty book borrowing, periodical check-out policies, and library hours.

LOST AND FOUND

Institutional policies and practices for turning in lost materials to campus authorities should be included here.

MAIL

Mailbox procedures for providing first-class and campus mail to part-time faculty members should be provided here.

PARKING

Part-time faculty should be given specific information on their rights to park on campus. If reimbursement is provided for parking expenses, these procedures should be included here.

PART-TIME FACULTY ABSENCE FROM CLASS

A statement similar to the following is useful in this section of the handbook:

- Classes will meet and be taught as scheduled and will be canceled only as a last resort.

- It is the responsibility of the part-time faculty member to notify the departmental chairperson and/or [other administrative entity considered appropriate] as soon as possible whenever a late arrival or an absence is necessary.

- Provision for class coverage in the absence of the part-time faculty member is the responsibility of the [administrative person responsible for this task].

- The various levels of class coverage are listed below and depend on the circumstances of the absence.

- The class will be taught or an examination, if scheduled, will be given.

- The class will meet, roll will be taken, and the class will be dismissed to pursue further research or written work already assigned.

- The class will meet, roll will be taken, directions will be given, and the class will be dismissed.

- As a last resort, the class will be canceled.

SMOKING, EATING, AND DRINKING

A statement similar to the following is useful in this section of the handbook:

Smoking is prohibited throughout the institution in the following areas: classrooms, elevators, laboratories, studios, auditoriums, restrooms, locker rooms, gymnasiums, swimming pools, and special-purpose classrooms. Smoking is also prohibited in all other rooms where *No Smoking* signs are posted. Smoking is permitted in other areas of the campus and leased facilities unless posted to the contrary. Eating and drinking are not permitted in classrooms whether or not a class is in session. It is the instructor's responsibility to see that these regulations are enforced.

STUDENT CONDUCT

A statement similar to the following is useful in this section of the handbook:

This institution can make its maximum contribution as an institution of higher learning only if high standards of courtesy, integrity, and accomplishment are demanded.

STUDENT FINANCIAL AID

Information about student financial aid should be inserted here, but only as much as is necessary to permit the part-time faculty member to refer someone to the appropriate office.

STUDENT RECORDS

Part-time faculty members should know how to obtain student records. Necessary information should be included here.

TEXTBOOK DESK COPIES

Procedures for obtaining desk copies of textbooks should be supplied here.

TEXTBOOK SELECTION PROCEDURES

Policies and procedures concerning who selects texts must be clarified.

WITHDRAWALS

Institutional policies and procedures concerning withdrawals from classes should be included in the handbook.

Bibliography

ABEL, EMILY. "The View from the Bottom: The Impact of Proposition 13 on Part-Time Faculty." Paper presented at the Annual Conference of the Modern Languages Association, San Francisco, CA, December 29, 1979.

————. *Terminal Degrees: The Job Crisis in Higher Education.* New York: Praeger, 1984.

ACADEMY FOR EDUCATIONAL DEVELOPMENT. *A Survey of Faculty Personnel Practices at 32 Urban Community Colleges; A Report to the Board of Trustees of the City Colleges of Chicago.* New York: Academy for Educational Development, 1976.

AMERICAN ASSOCIATION OF UNIVERSITY PROFESSORS. *Part-Time Faculty Series.* Washington, D.C.: AAUP, 1978.

ANDES, JOHN. "A Study of Part-Time Faculty in West Virginia Institutions of Higher Education." Photocopied. Morgantown, West Virginia, 1981.

ANGELL, GEORGE W., EDWARD P. KELLY, JR. AND ASSOCIATES. *Handbook of Faculty Bargaining.* San Francisco; Jossey-Bass, 1977.

159

ASSOCIATION OF AMERICAN COLLEGES. *Part-Time Faculty Employment: Project on the Status and Education of Women.* Washington, D.C.: Assocation of American Colleges, 1976.

BAUER, W. K. "Adjunct Professors: Appropriate and Inappropriate Personnel Policies and Procedures." *Journal of CUPA,* 30 (Winter 1979): 17–53.

BEHRENDT, R. L., AND MICHAEL H. PARSONS. "Evaluation of Part-Time Faculty." *New Directions for Community Colleges,* 41 (1983): 33–43.

BONHAM, G. W. "Part-Time Faculty: A Mixed Blessing." *Change,* 14 (April 1982): 10–11.

BOWEN, HOWARD R., AND JACK H. SCHUSTER. "Outlook for the Academic Profession," *Academe* (71) September-October, 1985, 9–15.

BRAMLETT, R., AND R. C. RODRIGUEZ. "Part-Time Faculty, Full-Time Concern." *Community and Junior College Journal,* 53 (December 1982–January 1983): 40–41.

BROWN, GRACE. "Part-Time Faculty Effectiveness: Fulfilling the Need." Paper presented at the National Policy Conference on Urban Community Colleges in Transition, Detroit, MI, March 1982.

Clark Technical College Adjunct Faculty Handbook. Springfield, OH: Clark Technical College, 1977.

COHEN, ARTHUR M., AND FLORENCE B. BRAWER. *The Two Year College Instructor Today.* New York: Praeger, 1977.

DAVIDSON, W., AND S. KLINE. "How to Get Two Experienced Teachers for the Price of One." *American School Board Journal,* 164 (September 1977): 35–36.

DOUGLASS, JOEL, AND LISA FLANZRAICH. *Collective Bargaining in Higher Education and the Professions, Bibliography No. 10.* New York: Bernard Baruch College National Center for the Study of Collective Bargaining in Higher Education and the Professions, 1982.

EMMET, THOMAS A., HOWARD P. TUCKMAN, BARBARA H. TUCKMAN, JOHN ANDES, RICHARD BAGWELL AND IONE ELIOF. *1981 Current Issues in Higher Education, No. 4: Part-Time Faculty in Colleges and Universities.* Washington, D.C.: American Association for Higher Education, 1981.

Faculty Handbook, 1981–1982. Berkeley, CA: Peralta Community College System, 1981.

FLANDERS, JANE. "The Use and Abuse of Part-Time Faculty." *Bulletin of the Association of Departments of Foreign Languages,* 8 (September 1976): 49–52.

FLYNN, THOMAS E. "Permanent Temporary Community College Teachers and the Due Process Clause." *Pacific Law Journal,* 11 (July 1980): 993–1017.

FORTUNATO, RAY T., AND D. G. WADDELL. *Personnel Administration in Higher Education.* San Francisco: Jossey-Bass, 1981.

FRIEDLANDER, JACK. "An ERIC Review: Instructional Practices of Part-Time and Full-Time Faculty." *Community College Review,* 6 (Winter 1979): 65–72.

FRYER, THOMAS W., JR. "Designing New Personnel Policies: The Permanent Part-Time Faculty Member." *Journal of the College and University Personnel Association,* 28 (Spring 1977): 14–21.

GAPPA, JUDITH M. "Employing Part-Time Faculty: Thoughtful Approaches to Continuing Problems." *AAHE Bulletin,* (October 1984): 3–7.

———. "Part-Time Faculty: Higher Education at a Crossroads." *Association for the Study of Higher Education-Clearinghouse on Higher Education, Higher Education Report No. 3,* 1984. pp. 1–2.

GARBARINO, JOSEPH W. *Faculty Bargaining.* New York: McGraw-Hill, 1975.

GOETSCH, D. L. "Tips for Part-Time Teachers," *Vocational Education,* 57 (June 1982): pp. 42–43.

GOWIN, D. B., AND GEORGE H. DAIGNEAULT. *The Part-Time College Teacher.* Brookline, MA: Center for the Study of Liberal Education for Adults, 1961.

GUTHRIE-MORSE, B. "Utilization of Part-Time Faculty." *Community College Frontiers,* 7 (Spring 1979): pp. 8–17.

HADDAD, MARGARET, AND MARY ELLEN DICKENS. "Competencies for Part-Time Faculty—The First Step." *Community and Junior College Journal,* 49 (November 1978): 22–24.

HAMMONS, JIM. "Adjunct Faculty: Another Look," *Community College Frontiers,* 9 (Winter 1981): 46–53.

HEAD, RONALD B. *Legal Issues Relating to a Part-Time Employment, Occasional Paper Series No. 6.* Charlottesville: University of Virginia Center for Higher Education, 1979.

HEAD, RONALD B., AND DAVID W. LESLIE. "Bargaining Unit Status of Part-Time Faculty." *Journal of Law and Education,* 8 (July 1979): 361–78.

HINE, P. A., AND J. C. LATACK. "Paradox of the Part-Time Professional." *Journal of the National Association for Women Deans, Administrators and Counselors,* 15 (January 16, 1978): 98–101.

HOENNINGER, RONALD, AND RICHARD A. BLACK. "Neglect of a Species." *Community and Junior College Journal,* 49 (November 1978): 25–27.

HOFFMAN, JOHN R. "The Use and Abuse of Part-Time Instructors." *Community Services Catalyst,* 10 (1980): 12–18.

HOFFMAN, JOHN R., AND P. A. POOL. "Part-Time Faculty: Their Own Needs Assessment." *Life-Long Learning: The Adult Years,* 2 (April 1979): 26–27.

HOWE, RICHARD. "Tenure Policies and Practices: A Summary." *Journal of the College and University Personnel Association,* 31 (Fall–Winter 1980): 18–31.

JOHNSON, C. "Vocational Education Without Higher Costs?" *Momentum,* 8 (May 1977): 16–17.

LANDERS, MARILYN G. "Part-Time Faculty: Their Responsibilities and Their Effectiveness." Excerpted from the Annual Report to the Texas Association of Junior and Community College Instructional Administrators by the Research Committee, June 1979.

LESLIE, DAVID W. *Employing Part-Time Faculty.* San Francisco: Jossey-Bass, 1978.

———. "Part Time Faculty: Legal and Collective Bargaining Issues." *AAHE Bulletin,* 37 (October 1984): 8–12.

LESLIE, DAVID W., AND R. B. HEAD. "Part-Time Faculty Rights." *Educational Record,* 60 (Winter 1979): 46–67.

LESLIE, DAVID W., AND D. J. IKENBERRY. "Collective Bargaining and Part-Time Faculty: Contract Content." *Journal of College and University Personnel Association,* 30 (Fall 1979): 18–26.

LESLIE, DAVID W., SAMUEL E. KILLIAMS, AND G. MANNY GUNNE. *Part-Time Faculty in American Higher Education.* New York: Praeger, 1982.

LOMBARDI, J. *Part-Time Faculty in Community Colleges. Topical Paper No. 54.* Los Angeles: ERIC Clearinghouse for Junior Colleges, 1975.

McDANIEL, WALTER A., AND PHILIP T. GULLO. *Faculty Retraining for Lateral Transfer: An Alternative to Reduction in Force in Community Colleges. A Study and Progress Report.* Los Angeles: Pepperdine University, 1978.

McLeod, D., and C. Kenny. "ADE Debates." *ADE Bulletin,* 66 (Winter 1980): 34–36.

Moodie, C. L. R. "Overuse of Part-Time Faculty Members." *Chronicle of Higher Education,* 20 (March 10, 1980): 72.

Norman, Mary M. "Advice and Recommendations: Improving the Work Environment for Part-Timers." *AAHE Bulletin,* (October 1984): 13–14.

Padgett, Suzanne C., and Raymond E. Schultz. *Survival Skills for Part-Time Faculty at Pima College's Community Campus.* Tucson: Pima Community College, 1979.

Parson, Michael H., ed. *Using Part-Time Faculty Effectively. New Directions for Community Colleges, No. 30.* San Francisco: Jossey-Bass, 1980.

Part-Time Faculty Handbook. Hagerstown, MD. Hagerstown Junior College, 1975.

Part-Time Faculty Handbook, 1975–1976. Rockville, MD. Montgomery College, 1975.

Peek, George A. *Community Report on the Status of Women.* Tempe: Arizona State University, 1973.

Plosser, William D., and Joseph H. Hammel. *Temporary, Contract or Regular? A Report about Court Cases Involving the Issues of the Status of the Status and Pay of Part-Time Faculty in California Community Colleges.* Sacramento: California Community and Junior College Association, 1976.

Pollack, Art, and Robert L. Breuer. "The Eighties and Part-Time Faculty." *Community College Review,* 9 (Spring 1982): 58–62.

Potter, Richard H. "Part-Time Faculty: Employees or Contractors?" *Journal of the College and University Personnel Association,* 35 (Fall 1984): 22–27.

Report of the Task Force on Temporary Faculty. Long Beach: California State University and Colleges, 1977.

Ross, Harry A. "Policy Considerations for the Use of Part-Time Faculty in Public Community Colleges." Ed.D. dissertation, West Virginia University, 1982.

Sanchez, Bonnie M. "Part-Time Community College Instructors." *Community Services Catalyst,* 10 (Spring–Summer 1980): 27–29.

Schall, Stanley L *Evening and Part Time Faculty Handbook.* Los Angeles: Los Angeles City College, 1980.

SCHREIBMEIER, ALAN JOHN. "An Investigation of Part-Time Faculty Staff Development in Public Community Colleges in the United States." Ph.D. dissertation, University of Texas at Austin, 1980.

SELDING, PETER. *How Colleges Evaluate Professors.* Croton-on-Hudson: Blythe, Pennington, 1975.

SMITH, MILTON L. *Part-Time Faculty in Private Junior Colleges.* San Marcos, Southwest Texas State University, 1981.

SPOFFORD, T. "Field Hands of Academe." *Change,* 11 (November–December 1979): pp. 14–16.

STERN, CAROL SIMPSON, JESSE H. CHOPER, MARY W. GRAY AND ROBERT J. WOLFSON, "The Status of Part-Time Faculty." *Academe: Bulletin of the AAUP,* 67 (February–March 1981): 29–39.

"Tenure at Comprehensive Universities and Colleges." *Journal of the College and University Personnel Association,* 31 (Fall–Winter 1980): 58–83.

TUCKMAN, HOWARD P. "Part-Time Faculty: Some Suggestions of Policy." *Change,* 13 (Janurary–February 1981): pp. 8–10.

TUCKMAN, HOWARD P. *Publication, Teaching and the Academic Reward Structure.* New York: Lexington Press, 1976.

———. "Who Is Part-Time in Academe?" *AAUP Bulletin,* 64 (December 1978): 305–15.

TUCKMAN, HOWARD P., AND JAIME CALDWELL. "The Reward Structure for Part-Timers in Academe." *Journal of Higher Education,* 50 (November 1979): 745–760.

——— JAIME CALDWELL AND WILLIAM VOGLER, "Exchange on Part-Time Employment," *American Sociologist;* 13 (November 1978): 184–195.

———. "Faculty Skills and Salary Structure in Academe: A Market Perspective," *American Economic Review;* 67 (September 1977): pp. 692–702.

TUCKMAN, HOWARD P., JAMES GAPINSKI, AND JAIME CALDWELL. "Wage Rates of Part-Timers in Higher Education: A Preliminary Inquiry." *Proceedings of the American Statistical Association,* (December 1977): pp. 507–511.

TUCKMAN, HOWARD P., AND DAVID KATZ. "Estimation of Relative Elasticities of Substitution and Relative Compensation for Part-time Faculty." *Economics of Education Review;* (Summer 1981) pp. 359–366.

———. "Displacement of Full-Timers by Part-Timers: A Model For

Projection." *Economics of Education Review,* 3 (Winter 1983): pp. 85–90.

TUCKMAN, HOWARD P., AND BARBARA TUCKMAN. "Sex-Discrimination among Part-Timers at Two-Year Institutions." 6 *Academe,* (Spring 1980): pp. 20–25.

———. "Who Are the Part-Timers and What are Colleges Doing for Them?" Part-Time Faculty in Colleges and Universities, 1981 Current Issues in Higher Education. Washington, D.C. American Association for Higher Education. 1981: pp. 4–8.

———. "The Labor Market for Part-Time Faculty at Business Schools." *Quarterly Review of Economics and Business: Journal of the Midwest Economics Association,* 24 (Autumn 1984): 95–103.

TUCKMAN, HOWARD P., AND WILLIAM VOGLER. "The 'Part' in Part-Time Wages." *AAUP Bulletin,* 64 (Summer 1978): 70–77.

———. "The Fringes of a Fringe Group: Part-Timers in Academe." *Part-Time Faculty Series,* Washington, D.C.: AAUP, 1978, pp. 40–52.

WILSON, LOGAN. *The Academic Man: A Study in the Sociology of a Profession.* New York: Oxford University Press, 1942.

———. *American Academics.* New York: Oxford University Press, 1979.

ZANDY, JANET. "The Part-Time Professor." *Upstate Magazine* of the Rochester, NY, *Sunday Democrat and Chronicle,* (December 9, 1984): 6–10.

Index

Index